W9-DAW-709

Walch Hands-on Science Series

Rocks and Minerals

by Barry Fried and Michael McDonnell

illustrated by Lloyd Birmingham

Project editors: Joel Beller and Carl Raab

WALCH PUBLISHING®

User's Guide
to
Walch Reproducible Books

As part of our general effort to provide educational materials that are as practical and economical as possible, we have designated this publication a "reproducible book." The designation means that purchase of the book includes purchase of the right to limited reproduction of all pages on which this symbol appears:

Here is the basic Walch policy: We grant to individual purchasers of this book the right to make sufficient copies of reproducible pages for use by all students of a single teacher. This permission is limited to a single teacher and does not apply to entire schools or school systems, so institutions purchasing the book should pass the permission on to a single teacher. Copying of the book or its parts for resale is prohibited.

Any questions regarding this policy or requests to purchase further reproduction rights should be addressed to:

Permissions Editor
J. Weston Walch, Publisher
P.O. Box 658
Portland, Maine 04104-0658

1   2   3   4   5   6   7   8   9   10
ISBN 0-8251-3935-X

Contents

To the Teacher

This is one in a series of hands-on science activities for middle school and early high school students. A recent survey of middle school students conducted by the National Science Foundation (NSF) found that

- more than half listed science as their favorite subject.
- more than half wanted more hands-on activities.
- 90 percent stated that the best way for them to learn science was to do experiments themselves.

The books in this series seek to capitalize on that NSF survey. These books are not texts but supplements. They offer hands-on, fun activities that will turn some students on to science. You and your students should select which activities are to be carried out. All of the activities need not be done. Pick and choose those activities that best meet the needs of your students. All of these activities can be done in school, and some can be done at home. The authors are teachers, and the activities have been field tested in a public middle school and/or high school.

Students will need only basic, standard scientific equipment that can be found in most middle and high school science laboratories. The activities range from the simple (How Are Crystals Created?) to the difficult (How Do We Use Rocks to Examine Geologic History?). There is something for every student.

THE ACTIVITIES CAN BE USED:

- to provide hands-on experiences pertaining to textbook content.
- to give verbally limited children a chance to succeed and gain extra credit.
- as the basis for class or school science fair projects or for other science competitions.
- to involve students in science club activities.
- as homework assignments.
- to involve parents in their child's science education and experiences.

The students will discover the special properties of rocks and minerals and how scientists use these properties to learn about the formation of the planet and the evolution of life on earth. Hands-on activities explain why we use rocks to examine geological history, how rocks and minerals weather, how different types of rocks form, and what we learn about the evolution of life from fossils.

Each activity has a Teacher Resource section that includes, besides helpful hints and suggestions, a scoring rubric, quiz questions, and Internet connections for those students who wish to go further and carry out the follow-up activities. Instructional objectives and the National Science Standards that apply to each activity are provided to help you meet state and local expectations.

How Can We Determine the Density of Regularly Shaped Objects?

 INSTRUCTIONAL OBJECTIVES

Students will be able to

- record and analyze data.
- measure the mass and volume of regularly shaped objects.
- measure the density of regularly shaped objects using mathematics.

 NATIONAL SCIENCE STANDARDS ADDRESSED

Students demonstrate an understanding of

- properties of matter, such as density.

Students demonstrate scientific inquiry and problem-solving skills by

- working in teams to collect and share information and ideas.
- identifying the outcomes of an investigation.

Students demonstrate effective scientific communication by

- representing data and results in multiple ways.

Students demonstrate competence with the tools and techniques of science by

- using tools and technology to observe and measure objects directly.

 MATERIALS

- Triple beam balance scale
- Aluminum block
- Aluminum cube
- Wooden block
- Water
- Graduated cylinder
- Centimeter ruler

HELPFUL HINTS AND DISCUSSION

Time frame: One or two class periods
Structure: Cooperative learning groups of three students
Location: In class

You can obtain the materials needed from science supply companies. Demonstrate the workings of the triple beam balance before permitting students to perform this experiment. Teach the concept of density.

ADAPTATIONS FOR HIGH AND LOW ACHIEVERS

High Achievers: Encourage these students to carry out the Follow-up Activities. They should also help the low achievers.

Low Achievers: These students should work with the high achievers and the teacher. These students may need help using the triple beam balance and grasping the concept of density.

SCORING RUBRIC

Full credit should be given to those students who accurately record observations and provide correct answers in full sentences to the questions. Extra credit may be given if any of the Follow-up Activities are completed satisfactorily.

 **INTERNET TIE-INS**
http://www2.hn.psu.edu/faculty/dmencer/density.html
http://tqd.advanced.org/2690/exper/exp25.htm
http://www.calsur.com/calsur/ScienceProjects/EggFloat

 QUIZ
1. What is the density of a 50-gram cube that measures 3 cm on one side?
2. Outline the procedure for determining the density of 50 ml of water.
3. If an object that has a density of 5 grams per cubic centimeter is split in half, how will the density of the two halves compare to the density of the original piece?

How Can We Determine the Density of Regularly Shaped Objects?

 BEFORE YOU BEGIN

Many people believe that heavy objects sink while light objects float. This is not always the case. After all, icebergs weighing several tons float, but pennies, which weigh only a few grams, sink. We use a concept called **density** to explain whether or not an object sinks or floats.

Two steps are necessary to find the density of an object. First, you must determine the mass and volume of an object. **Mass** is the amount of matter in an object. It is measured in kilograms. **Volume** is the amount of space an object takes up. Volume is measured in liters or milliliters. Once you have determined the mass and volume of an object, you can calculate its density by using this equation:

$$\text{Density} = \frac{\text{Mass}}{\text{Volume}} \quad (D = M/V).$$

Objects that are less dense than an equal volume of water will float. Objects that are more dense than an equal volume of water will sink. An iceberg is less dense than an equal volume of water, and therefore it floats. A penny is denser than an equal volume of water, and therefore the penny sinks. Objects, like icebergs, that are filled with air and have a large volume for their mass usually float.

Density is one of the most important physical properties on earth. It enables molten rock to flow up into volcanoes. It affects the movement of ocean currents and the rising and sinking of air. Without density there would be no weather, earthquakes, or volcanoes.

In this first of two activities, you will use several different methods to measure the density of regularly shaped objects and the density of water. This will give you a better feel for the concept of density.

 MATERIALS

- Triple beam balance scale
- Aluminum block
- Aluminum cube
- Wooden block
- Water
- Graduated cylinder
- Centimeter ruler

 PROCEDURE

To carry out this activity in an organized manner, assign specific tasks to each member of your group. One member should use the triple beam balance to measure the mass of the objects. Another should measure the volume of the objects with a centimeter ruler. The third group member should collect and analyze data. Be sure to take turns for each of the three objects, so that each group member is able to perform all three activities.

1. Have the group member assigned to determine the volume of the aluminum cube use the centimeter ruler to measure its length, width, and height. Then determine the cube's volume using this formula: Volume = Length × Width × Height.

(continued)

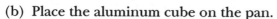

How Can We Determine the Density of Regularly Shaped Objects? *(continued)*

2. The student assigned to the triple beam balance should measure the mass of the aluminum cube by doing the following:

   (a) Zero the triple beam balance by making sure that all the riders are at zero and by using the leveling screw below the pan to make sure the pointer is at zero.

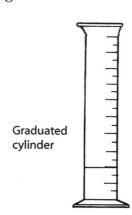

Triple beam balance

   (b) Place the aluminum cube on the pan.

   (c) Start moving the largest rider one notch at a time. When the pointer drops below the *0* mark, move the rider one notch back to the left.

   (d) Do the same for the rider on the middle beam.

   (e) Move the front or smaller rider until the pointer is at *0.*

   (f) Record the riders of the three beams to the nearest tenth of a gram (g). This is the mass of the aluminum cube.

   (g) Return the riders to zero.

3. The student assigned to collect and analyze the data should first record the mass and volume of the aluminum cube in Data Table 1 in the Data Collection and Analysis section. Then he or she should determine the density of the aluminum cube by using the formula:

$$\text{Density} = \frac{\text{Mass}}{\text{Volume}}.$$

4. Switch roles and repeat steps 1 through 3 using the aluminum bar. Be sure to enter the information in Data Table 1.

5. Switch roles again and repeat steps 1 through 3, this time using the wooden block. Complete Data Table 1 for the wooden block.

6. Your group will now determine the density of water by doing the following:

   (a) Obtain an empty graduated cylinder and find its mass using the triple beam balance (use the same technique as in step 2).

   (b) Pour a volume of 30 ml of water into the graduated cylinder, and enter this volume in Data Table 1. Place the filled cylinder on the triple beam balance and determine its mass.

   (c) Finally, subtract the mass of the empty graduated cylinder from the filled cylinder to determine the mass in grams of the water alone. Enter the mass of water in Data Table 1.

Graduated cylinder

   (d) Determine the density of water by using the formula from step 3. Enter this density in Data Table 1.

(continued)

Name _____ Date _____

 DATA COLLECTION AND ANALYSIS

TABLE 1: DENSITY OF REGULARLY SHAPED OBJECTS AND WATER (INDIVIDUAL)

Object	Mass	Volume	Density
Aluminum cube (1)			
Aluminum bar (2)			
Wooden block (3)			
Water (4)			

CONCLUDING QUESTIONS

1. Compare the densities of the aluminum cube and the aluminum block. Explain your results.

   _____

   _____

   _____

   _____

2. Which of these objects should float in a container of water? Why? Perform the experiment to prove your answer. _____

   _____

   _____

   _____

   _____

3. Explain why ships can float. _____

   _____

   _____

   _____

Follow-up Activities

1. Create and perform an experiment to determine the density of cylindrical and triangular objects using the methods introduced in this activity.
2. Create and perform an experiment to measure changes in the density of water as salt is added. Start with a fresh-water sample and continually add salt until no more will dissolve.

How Can We Determine the Density of Irregularly Shaped Objects?

 INSTRUCTIONAL OBJECTIVES

Students will be able to

- record and analyze data.
- measure the mass and volume of irregularly shaped objects.
- determine the density of irregularly shaped objects.

 NATIONAL SCIENCE STANDARDS ADDRESSED

Students demonstrate an understanding of

- properties of matter, such as density.

Students demonstrate scientific inquiry and problem-solving skills by

- working in teams to collect and share information and ideas.
- identifying the outcomes of an investigation.

Students demonstrate effective scientific communication by

- representing data and results in multiple ways.

Students demonstrate competence with the tools and techniques of science by

- using tools and technology to observe and measure objects directly.

 MATERIALS

- Triple beam balance scale
- Four mineral samples (calcite, magnetite, pyrite, and sulfur)
- Glass marble
- Lead sinker
- Water
- Graduated cylinder

HELPFUL HINTS AND DISCUSSION

Time frame: One or two class periods
Structure: Cooperative learning groups of three students
Location: In class

Demonstrate how to use the triple beam balance before permitting students to perform this experiment. Review the concept of density. Students should be taught to slide the objects gently into the graduated cylinder at an angle so that the glass will not break. You may want to have students perform this activity near a sink under your supervision so that they can easily clean their work stations. Teach students how to read the meniscus in a graduated cylinder. The mineral samples need to be small enough to fit inside the graduated cylinder easily.

ADAPTATIONS FOR HIGH AND LOW ACHIEVERS

High Achievers: Encourage these students to carry out all Follow-up Activities. They should also help low achievers.

Low Achievers: These students should work with the high achievers and the teacher. These students may need help using the triple beam balance and grasping the concept of density.

SCORING RUBRIC

Full credit should be given to those students who accurately record observations and provide correct answers in full sentences to the questions. Extra credit may be given if any of the Follow-up Activities are completed satisfactorily.

 **INTERNET TIE-INS**
http://www2.hn.psu.edu/faculty/dmencer/density.html
http://tqd.advanced.org/2690/exper/exp25.htm
http://www.calsur.com/calsur/ScienceProjects/EggFloat

 QUIZ
1. Explain a method that you could use to determine your volume.
2. Which method of determining volume (mathematics or water displacement) would be most useful for rocks and minerals that we find in the real world? Explain your answer.

Name _____ Date _____

How Can We Determine the Density of Irregularly Shaped Objects?

  BEFORE YOU BEGIN

In the previous activity, you measured the mass and volume of several regularly shaped objects. Then you determined their density. It is easy to determine the mass and volume of **regularly** shaped objects. We can easily measure their mass using a triple beam balance, and since they have a regular shape, we can determine their volume using a mathematical formula. This is not the case for **irregularly** shaped objects. We can still measure their mass using the triple beam balance. However, there is no mathematical formula to determine their volume. We can, however, use another method—water displacement.

If you have ever filled a bathtub to the top and then gotten in, you know that some of the water spilled out onto the floor. This is the water your body has replaced. People have known for thousands of years that when an object—your body or anything else—is placed in water, it will **displace** some of the water. It turns out that the volume of water displaced exactly equals the volume of the object placed in the water. In other words, when an object is placed in water, it will force an equal volume of water out.

In this second of a series of two activities, you will measure the volume of irregularly shaped objects using the water displacement method. Then you will determine the object's mass using a triple beam balance. Using these data, you can then determine the density of these objects.

 MATERIALS

- Triple beam balance scale
- Four mineral samples (calcite, magnetite, pyrite, and sulfur)
- Glass marble
- Lead sinker
- Water
- Graduated cylinder

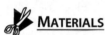 **PROCEDURE**

To carry out this activity in an organized manner, assign specific tasks to each member of your group. One member should use the triple beam balance to measure the mass of each object. Another should measure the volume of the objects using the water displacement method. The third group member should collect and analyze data. Be sure to take turns for each of the six objects, so that each group member is able to perform all three activities twice.

1. First, use the triple beam balance to measure the mass of each object by doing the following:

   (a) Zero the triple beam balance by making sure that all the riders are at zero and by using the leveling screw below the pan to make sure the pointer is at zero.

   (b) Place the object on the pan.

   (c) Start moving the largest rider one notch at a time. When the pointer drops below the *0* mark, move the rider one notch back to the left.

   (d) Do the same for the rider on the middle beam.

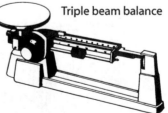
Triple beam balance

(continued)

How Can We Determine the Density of Irregularly Shaped Objects? *(continued)*

(e) Move the front or smaller rider until the pointer is at *0*.

(f) Record the riders of the three beams to the nearest tenth of a gram (g). This is the mass of the object.

(g) Return the riders to zero.

2. Next, use the water displacement method to obtain the volume of each object by doing the following:

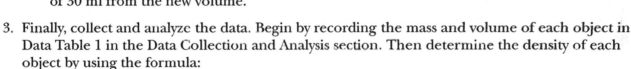

(a) Obtain an empty graduated cylinder and pour 30 ml of water into it.

(b) Holding the graduated cylinder at a slight angle, carefully slide in the object until it rests on the bottom of the cylinder. This should be done under the strict supervision of your teacher.

Graduated
cylinder

(c) Put the cylinder upright on a flat surface and read the new volume in the cylinder by bending until your eye is level with it. Make sure that your reading is at the bottom of the **meniscus**, the curved surface of the water in the cylinder.

(d) Determine the volume of each object by subtracting the initial volume of 30 ml from the new volume.

3. Finally, collect and analyze the data. Begin by recording the mass and volume of each object in Data Table 1 in the Data Collection and Analysis section. Then determine the density of each object by using the formula:

$$\text{Density} = \frac{\text{Mass}}{\text{Volume}}.$$

4. Select a member from your group to record your results on the class chart. Then, copy the chart into Table 2: Density of Irregularly Shaped Objects (Class Average). Finally, compute the average for each of the six objects.

 DATA COLLECTION AND ANALYSIS

TABLE 1: DENSITY OF IRREGULARLY SHAPED OBJECTS (INDIVIDUAL GROUP)

Object	Mass	Volume	Density
Mineral 1 (1)			
Mineral 2 (2)			
Mineral 3 (3)			
Mineral 4 (4)			
Glass marble (5)			
Lead sinker (6)			

(continued)

How Can We Determine the Density of Irregularly Shaped Objects? *(continued)*

TABLE 2: DENSITY OF IRREGULARLY SHAPED OBJECTS (CLASS AVERAGE)

Object									Average
	Group Number								
	1	2	3	4	5	6	7	8	
1									
2									
3									
4									
5									
6									

❓ CONCLUDING QUESTIONS

1. Assume you have an unknown liquid with a density of 3.0 grams per cubic centimeter. Name all objects used in this activity that would float in that liquid. _____
    _____
    _____
    _____

2. Lead is commonly used as a weight to make objects sink in water. Name two properties of lead that make it useful for this purpose. _____
    _____
    _____

3. You were given a ring. How can you determine if it is pure gold? _____
    _____
    _____

🔲 Follow-up Activities 🔲

1. Design and perform an experiment to determine the year in which the composition of pennies was changed from copper to zinc. (*Hint:* The change occurred between 1976 and 1993.)
2. Determine the density of three regularly shaped objects (wood block, aluminum cube, and aluminum block) using the water displacement method. Account for any differences that you find.

How Are Crystals Created?

 INSTRUCTIONAL OBJECTIVES

Students will be able to

- observe changes in crystalline structure.
- sketch the appearance of crystals over time.
- relate crystal structure to the formation of minerals.

 NATIONAL SCIENCE STANDARDS ADDRESSED

Students demonstrate an understanding of

- properties of earth materials, such as rocks and soils.
- the structure of atoms.
- big ideas and unifying concepts, such as change and constancy.

Students demonstrate effective scientific communication by

- representing data in multiple ways, such as drawings and artwork.

 MATERIALS

- One cup water (distilled water works best)
- From 1.5 to 2 cups of granulated sugar
- One tall, empty beaker or jar
- One popsicle stick
- One paper clip
- Thin string
- Heat-resistant beaker (Pyrex®)
- Ⓢ Hot plate
- Potholder

Ⓢ = Safety icon

HELPFUL HINTS AND DISCUSSION

Time frame: One week
Structure: Individuals or cooperative learning groups
Location: In class

In this activity, students will investigate the creation of sugar crystals during a one-week period. They will sketch the change in appearance of the crystals during this period and answer questions based on their observations. Students can then relate what they have observed in this experiment to the appearance of mineral crystals. In later activities, students will relate these crystalline structures to the physical properties exhibited by those minerals that determine a mineral's physical makeup. Ⓢ **Make sure that hot plates are used only under your supervision.**

ADAPTATIONS FOR HIGH AND LOW ACHIEVERS

High Achievers: Encourage these students to carry out all Follow-up Activities. Allow these students access to different mineral samples so that they can investigate the effect of crystalline structure on the physical properties of a mineral.

Low Achievers: These students should work in cooperative learning groups or carry out their investigations with the help of higher-achieving students and/or the teacher.

SCORING RUBRIC

Full credit should be given to students who carry out the activity, complete the sketches, and complete the Follow-up Activities.

 INTERNET TIE-INS

http://agcwww.bio.ns.ca/schools/rocks/cardinell_1.html
http://www.hamptonresearch.com/GIC.html
http://www.geolab.unc.edu/Petunia/IgMetAtlas/mainmenu.html

 **QUIZ**

1. How can you prove that the sugar did not vanish when it was dissolved in the water?
2. What process allowed the water to leave the jar, but not the sugar?
3. What visible form did the crystals take?

Name _____   Date _____

How Are Crystals Created?

 BEFORE YOU BEGIN

Minerals are naturally occurring, inorganic materials that exist in a **crystalline** form. This crystalline form usually results when liquid rock (**magma**) from deep within the Earth comes to the surface and cools. Magma is made of different minerals, and as magma cools, atoms of the different minerals begin to align themselves into orderly arrangements called **crystals**. This orderly arrangement of atoms determines a mineral's shape, appearance, hardness, and many other physical properties. Slight differences in the orderly arrangement of atoms can have major effects on the physical properties of the minerals. For example, both diamonds and graphite are minerals composed of the element carbon. When carbon is placed under extreme pressure, the atoms align themselves into diamonds. If the pressure is less intense, then graphite is the result.

In this activity, you will sketch how common sugar crystallizes over a period of days. While you sketch, notice how the crystal form of sugar determines the resulting shape, size, and appearance of the grains. You will then relate what you have observed to the formation of minerals on Earth.

 ## MATERIALS

- One cup water (distilled water works best)
- From 1.5 to 2 cups of granulated sugar
- One tall, empty beaker or jar
- One popsicle stick
- One paper clip

- Thin string
- Heat-resistant beaker (Pyrex)
-  Hot plate
- Potholder

 = Safety icon

 ## PROCEDURE

1.  **Under the careful supervision of your teacher or another adult**, pour the water into the heat-resistant beaker and carefully heat it on the hot plate until the water boils. **Then turn off the heat.**

2. Gradually add the sugar, a spoonful at a time, to the hot water. Stir after each addition to dissolve. Continue adding sugar gradually until no more will dissolve in the water. If necessary, heat the solution to make it clear.

3. Let the solution cool a bit, and then, using a potholder, pour it into the other jar or beaker.  **Caution: If the solution is too hot, it might break the jar or beaker.**

4. Cut a length of string that is about 6 mm shorter than the height of the jar. Attach a paper clip to one end of the string and tie the other end to the center of the popsicle stick.

5. Rub a few grains of sugar along the string.

6. Slowly lower the string into the solution, making sure that the paper clip does not touch the bottom of the jar. Rest the popsicle stick across the rim.

(continued)

How Are Crystals Created? *(continued)*

Procedure 6

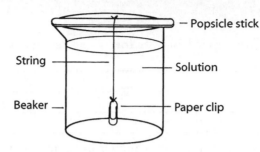

7. Let the solution cool and allow it to rest undisturbed for several days. Place it in a location designated by your teacher.

8. **Carefully** remove the string from the solution for a short period of time. Quickly sketch the appearance of the paper clip. Return the string and paper clip to the solution. Do this every day for seven days.

DATA COLLECTION AND ANALYSIS

Day One	Day Two

Day Three	Day Four

Day Five	Day Six

Day Seven

(continued)

How Are Crystals Created? *(continued)*

CONCLUDING QUESTIONS

1. Describe the change in the paper clip over the seven-day period. _____

   _____

   _____

   _____

   _____

2. What physical properties of a mineral are determined by its crystalline structure? _____

   _____

   _____

   _____

▨ **Follow-up Activities** ▨

1. Repeat the experiment by first removing the string of crystals that formed around the paper clip from the jar or beaker. Then, reheat the solution and gently place your original popsicle stick, string, and sugar crystals back in the jar/beaker. Predict what will happen after another seven days. What actually happened?

2. Connect to http://www.hamptonresearch.com/GIC.html and follow the directions to create crystals with different chemicals. (✋) **This should be done under the strict supervision of your teacher or another adult!**

How Do We Study the Crystal Structure of Salt?

 INSTRUCTIONAL OBJECTIVES

Students will be able to

- identify and characterize salt compounds.
- demonstrate extracting salt compounds from soil and from seawater.
- prepare a solution of dissolved minerals for identification.
- examine and describe the structure of salt crystals.

 NATIONAL SCIENCE STANDARDS ADDRESSED

Students demonstrate an understanding of

- properties of earth materials, such as rocks and minerals.
- properties and changes in matter, such as solubility.
- structure and properties of matter, such as bonding and molecular interaction.

Students demonstrate scientific inquiry and problem-solving skills by

- working in teams to collect and share information and ideas.
- using evidence from reliable sources to develop explanations.

Students demonstrate effective scientific communication by

- representing data and results in the form of tables.

Students demonstrate competence with the tools and techniques of science by

- using technology and tools, such as laboratory equipment.

 MATERIALS

- Sterilized soil sample or potting soil, seawater, table salt (NaCl)
- Halite and calcite specimens
- Tray kit containing a hand lens, spatula, filter paper, matches or striker, grease pencil
- Three large test tubes (15 mm × 125 mm)
- Three 50-ml Erlenmeyer flasks
- 50-ml graduated cylinder
- Test-tube rack
- Filter paper
- Rubber stoppers
- Three watch glasses or three evaporating dishes
- Ring stand, ring, and wire gauze
- Bunsen burner
- Paper towels
- Safety goggles

 = Safety icon

HELPFUL HINTS AND DISCUSSION

Time frame: One or two class periods
Structure: Cooperative learning groups of four students
Location: In class laboratory

Collect seawater, preferably algae free. To kill any growing organisms, heat the seawater to the boiling point before distributing it to students. For the soil samples, you should use soil from your local region or home potting soil. Large 2-inch square samples of halite and calcite can be purchased through major science supply companies. Be certain to prepare a model answer key for the correct crystalline array for each mineral salt. Crystals of halite should display a cubic shape, and calcite crystals should exhibit a rhomboid shape. A variety of salts will be present in seawater, and students should be aware that they will not necessarily be able to identify all of the salt crystals present. If the lesson is conducted in cooperative-group format, assign each group member one of the salt samples to prepare for each section of the exercise. Only clean glassware and distilled water should be used when preparing the samples for soluble minerals. **Safety procedures must be followed, particularly when using the alcohol lamp and the matches (or striker).**

<table>
<tr><td>

ADAPTATIONS FOR HIGH AND LOW ACHIEVERS

High Achievers: Encourage these students to complete the Follow-up Activities. They should also help the low achievers to perform many of the required tasks.

Low Achievers: These students should be in a cooperative learning group with high achievers and be given a more active role in performing many of the tasks. They should also be asked to help the teacher demonstrate the tasks performed in the activity.

</td><td>

SCORING RUBRIC

Full credit should be given to students who successfully conduct the activity in a safe manner, demonstrate proficiency in recording observations, and provide accurate, complete responses to the questions. Extra credit should be awarded to students who complete the Follow-up Activities.

</td></tr>
</table>

 **INTERNET TIE-INS**   http://www.saltinstitute.org/4.html
http://www.cals.cornell.edu/dept/flori/growon/salt.html

 QUIZ   1. What is the elemental composition of table salt?
2. Why don't you see salt in seawater?
3. How does the shape of a large sample of halite compare with smaller pieces viewed under the hand lens?

How Do We Study the Crystal Structure of Salt?

 BEFORE YOU BEGIN

Salt is something you probably use every day without stopping to think about what it really is. Did you know that table salt is a chemical compound called sodium chloride (NaCl)? It is composed of two elements: sodium metal (Na) and chlorine gas (Cl). Both of these are deadly to the human body in their natural state. However, when chemically combined, they form our most often used seasoning. The particular crystalline structure of a salt depends upon the arrangement of the atoms that make up the elements of that particular salt. Salts are found throughout many environments, including soils and, of course, the oceans. Even **freshwater** regions—including lakes, rivers, and streams—contain salt, but in much lower concentrations than the **saltwater** oceans. Agricultural scientists are particularly interested in the study of salts. Too much saltiness and specific salt compounds can severely damage soils and their crops. In this activity, you will examine the crystalline structure of salts. You will also extract salt compounds from seawater and from soil.

 MATERIALS

- Sterilized soil sample or potting soil, seawater, table salt (NaCl)
- Halite and calcite specimens
- Tray kit containing a hand lens, spatula, filter paper, matches or striker, grease pencil
- Three large test tubes (15mm × 125mm)
- Three 50-ml Erlenmeyer flasks
- 50-ml graduated cylinder
- Test-tube rack
- Filter paper

- Rubber stoppers
- Three watch glasses or three evaporating dishes
- Ring stand, ring, and wire gauze
- Bunsen burner
- Paper towels
- Safety goggles

 = Safety icon

 PROCEDURE

1. Obtain your testing samples and a tray kit from your teacher. **Be certain to inventory all of your supplies!**

2. Examine some table-salt crystals on a glass plate with a hand lens. Describe the structure of the crystals, and record your observations about their appearance in the appropriate place in Data Table 1 of the Data Collection and Analysis section.

3. Using a spatula, chip off a small fragment from the halite sample, and observe the shape of the fragment. Chip off a piece from the small fragment, and once again, observe the shape. Continue this procedure until the piece is extremely small and you need a hand lens to observe the halite particle. Record and sketch your results in the appropriate spaces in Data Table 1 of the Data Collection and Analysis section.

(continued)

How Do We Study the Crystal Structure of Salt? *(continued)*

4. Repeat step 3 for the calcite specimen. Record and sketch your results in the appropriate spaces in Data Table 1 of the Data Collection and Analysis section.

5. Prepare your table salt, soil, and seawater samples to be tested for the presence of soluble minerals by doing the following:

   (a) Label three test tubes for each sample to be tested.

   (b) Place approximately two centimeters (cm) of the **table salt** into its own test tube. Do the same for the **soil** sample. Add 10 milliliters (ml) of distilled water to each test tube, and stopper each test tube with a rubber stopper. Shake each test tube vigorously for 30 seconds to dissolve any soluble particles in your sample.

   (c) Place 10 ml of the **seawater** sample into its own test tube, and stopper the test tube with a rubber stopper.

   (d) Remove the stopper from each test tube. Pour your solution onto a piece of filter paper placed in a plastic funnel, held in place on a ring stand over a prelabeled 50 ml Erlenmeyer flask. Repeat for each test tube, using a different piece of filter paper for each one.

   (e) Allow each solution to drip completely through the filter paper into its own 50-ml Erlenmeyer flask. Then, cover the flasks with a rubber stopper or aluminum foil.

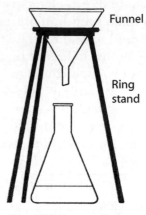

Funnel

Ring stand

50 ml Erlenmeyer flask

Procedure 5d

6. Separate out the dissolved minerals for each sample by doing the following:

   (a) Transfer each solution into a prelabeled watch glass or evaporating dish.

   (b) Place each watch glass or evaporating dish on the ring stand.

   (c) **Under the strict supervision of your teacher, carefully light a bunsen burner, and gently warm the solution to completely evaporate all of the water.**

   (d) Allow each solution to cool down completely before proceeding to the next step.

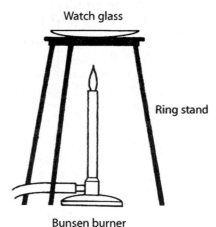

Watch glass

Ring stand

Bunsen burner

Procedure 6

7. Using a hand lens, examine each sample for dissolved minerals, and record your results in Data Table 2 of the Data Collection and Analysis section. Sketch any soluble mineral types you observe, and detail particular geometric shapes.

(continued)

Name _____   Date _____

 DATA COLLECTION AND ANALYSIS

DATA TABLE 1: STUDENT DESCRIPTIONS OF THE CRYSTAL SHAPES OF SALTS

Sample	Appearance of Crystal Shape	Sketch
Table salt		
Halite		
Calcite		

DATA TABLE 2: STUDENT DESCRIPTIONS OF SOLUBLE SALTS IN SEAWATER AND SOIL SAMPLES

Sample	Appearance of Soluble Salts	Sketch
Table salt		
Soil		
Seawater		

(continued)

How Do We Study the Crystal Structure of Salt? *(continued)*

❔ CONCLUDING QUESTIONS

1. Compare the shapes of halite, table salt, and calcite crystals. _____

_____

_____

_____

2. How can you find out if soil contains salts? _____

_____

_____

_____

3. Explain in your own words the procedure for isolating salts from substances containing salts.

_____

_____

_____

_____

▒ Follow-up Activities ▒

1. Salt (sodium chloride) is found in abundance in the United States. Most salt is excavated from mines. Some salt is extracted from our oceans. Research and write a report describing the process of removing salt from water, which is called **desalination**.

2. Describe how salt is used in food preservation.

How Can We Use Water to Identify Minerals?

 INSTRUCTIONAL OBJECTIVES

Students will be able to

- determine the specific gravity of a mineral sample.
- identify the mineral by its specific gravity.

 NATIONAL SCIENCE STANDARDS ADDRESSED

Students demonstrate an understanding of

- properties of earth materials, such as rocks and soils.

Students demonstrate scientific inquiry and problem-solving skills by

- working individually and in teams to collect and share information and ideas.

Students demonstrate competence with the tools and techniques of science by

- using technology and tools, such as laboratory equipment.

 MATERIALS

- Styrofoam cup
- Small stirring straws
- Modeling clay
- Triple beam balance scale
- Several mineral samples sized for student use (calcite, magnetite, galena, sulfur, feldspar, gypsum, and pyrite)
- Small beaker with graduated markings (ml)

HELPFUL HINTS AND DISCUSSION

Time frame: One class period
Structure: Individuals or cooperative learning groups
Location: In class

In this activity, students determine the specific gravity of several mineral samples. Several specific samples have been mentioned; however, you can use any number of different minerals. These minerals and others can be obtained from any major scientific supply house. It is also suggested that you obtain mineral samples sized for student use, since they are the easiest to work with. You may also opt to buy larger samples and crush them into different-sized pieces.

ADAPTATIONS FOR HIGH AND LOW ACHIEVERS

High Achievers: Encourage these students to carry out all Follow-up Activities.

Low Achievers: These students should work in cooperative learning groups or carry out their investigations with the help of a parent, a teacher, or another adult.

SCORING RUBRIC

Full credit should be given to students who carry out the activity independently, complete the sketches, and complete the Follow-up Activities.

 **INTERNET TIE-INS**
http://wgdb.sdvc.uwyo.edu/
http://mineral.galleries.com/Minerals/Density.htm
http://www.cci.unl.edu/SHU/SpGravityHW.html

 QUIZ
1. How would the specific gravity of gold change if it was cut in half?
2. How can you prove that the water in the beaker equals the volume of the mineral sample?
3. How can you identify a mineral based on its specific gravity?

How Can We Use Water to Identify Minerals?

 BEFORE YOU BEGIN

As you have learned, minerals owe their physical properties to the structure of their atoms and the alignment of these atoms to form crystals. Since the atoms of each mineral align differently, each mineral has different physical properties. You can use these differences to identify specific minerals. By using a property called specific gravity, you will be able to identify different minerals and their unique physical properties.

Specific gravity is determined by comparing the weight of a mineral to the weight of an equal volume of water. After weighing the mineral in the air, you will weigh the amount of water that the mineral displaces. This can be done by placing a small mineral sample in a cup of water with an overflow spout. The spout allows the amount of water displaced by the mineral sample to be collected. The overflowing water is equal in volume to the space taken up by the mineral. The space represents the mineral's volume. Since almost all minerals are denser than water, they will sink in a container of water, completely displacing their volume.

For instance, pure gold has a specific gravity of approximately 19.3. Since gold has a high specific gravity, it can easily be distinguished from other goldlike minerals. Testing for specific gravity is how people determined if they had found gold during the Gold Rush.

In this activity, you will use the concept of specific gravity to help identify seven minerals. You will discover that nonmetallic minerals usually have a low specific gravity and metals (like gold) have higher specific gravities.

 MATERIALS

- Styrofoam cup
- Small stirring straws
- Modeling clay
- Triple beam balance scale

- Several mineral samples sized for student use (calcite, magnetite, galena, sulfur, feldspar, gypsum, and pyrite)
- Small beaker with graduated markings (ml)

 PROCEDURE

1. Use the scissors to cut a small round hole in the Styrofoam cup, approximately one quarter of the way from the top.

2. Carefully cut the straw so that it is approximately 2.5 inches long. Place the straw in the hole that you cut into the cup. Make sure that the longer end sticks **outside** the cup. Using the modeling clay, create a waterproof seal on the outside of the cup around the straw.

3. Weigh the mineral sample on the triple beam balance and then weigh the empty beaker. Record both numbers in Data Table 1 in the Data Collection and Analysis section.

(continued)

How Can We Use Water to Identify Minerals? *(continued)*

4. Fill the Styrofoam cup with water up to the level of the lower surface of the straw. Then, place the small graduated beaker under the part of the straw sticking out from the cup.

5. Carefully place the mineral sample in the water so that no water splashes out of the cup. Some water will flow through the straw into the beaker.

6. Weigh the beaker with the overflow water in it. Record that value.

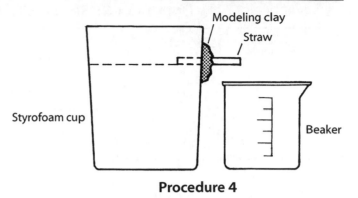

Procedure 4

7. Using the following formula, determine the specific gravity of the mineral sample:

$$\text{Specific Gravity} = \frac{\text{Weight of Mineral in Air}}{\text{Weight of an Equal Volume of Water}}.$$

8. Using Data Table 2 in the Data and Analysis section, determine the name of the mineral sample, and place this name in the appropriate place on Data Table 1.

9. Repeat steps 3–7 for each mineral sample. Remember to replace the water in the Styrofoam cup after each trial.

 DATA COLLECTION AND ANALYSIS

DATA TABLE 1

1 Name of Mineral	2 Weight of Mineral in Air (Grams)	3 Weight of Empty Beaker (Grams)	4 Weight of Beaker + Overflow Water (Grams)	5 Weight of Equal Volume of Water (Grams) (Col. 4–Col. 3)	6 Specific Gravity

(continued)

Name _____ Date _____

DATA TABLE 2: SPECIFIC GRAVITY OF SELECTED MINERALS

Mineral Name	Specific Gravity
Calcite	2.711
Gypsum	2.314–2.328
Galena	7.3–7.6
Feldspar	2.55
Pyrite	4.35
Magnetite	5.0

CONCLUDING QUESTIONS

1. Which minerals are easily distinguished by their specific gravity? Which ones are not? _____
_____
_____
_____
_____
_____

2. What factors make it easy to identify a mineral by its specific gravity? _____
_____
_____
_____

3. Why doesn't specific gravity have any units? What do the numbers actually mean?
_____
_____
_____
_____

Follow-up Activities

1. Determine the specific gravity of unknown minerals that come from your local area. Use a mineral identification chart or computer software program to identify them.

2. Using a rock hammer and **safety glasses**, reduce some of the samples to smaller pieces. Measure the specific gravity of as many pieces as possible. Determine if size affects specific gravity.

How Do We Determine the Hardness of Minerals?

 INSTRUCTIONAL OBJECTIVES

Students will be able to

- identify an "unknown" mineral through testing methods.
- observe and compare the hardness values of various minerals.
- interpret a mineral identification chart.

 NATIONAL SCIENCE STANDARDS ADDRESSED

Students demonstrate an understanding of

- properties of earth materials, such as rocks and minerals.
- characteristics of minerals, such as hardness.

Students demonstrate scientific inquiry and problem-solving skills by

- working in teams to collect and share information and ideas.
- determining the identity of an "unknown" mineral.

Students demonstrate effective scientific communication by

- representing data and results in the form of tables.

 MATERIALS

- Several numbered "unknown" mineral specimens (such as talc, feldspar, halite, gypsum, olivine, pyroxine, biotite, pyrite, quartz, calcite, hornblende, fluorite, galena)
- Tray kit containing a glass plate, a copper penny, and an iron nail
- Safety goggles

HELPFUL HINTS AND DISCUSSION

Time frame: One or two class periods, depending upon how many "unknown" samples are tested

Structure: Cooperative learning groups of four students

Location: In class

Use mineral identification kits or 2-inch square samples that can be purchased through major science supply companies. Randomly number the specimens, and distribute a variety of different samples to each student group. Be certain to prepare a separate answer key for each group. If the lesson is conducted in cooperative-group format, assign each group member a particular hardness test to perform. Ⓢ **Safety procedures must be followed, particularly when using the iron nail and the glass plate.**

ADAPTATIONS FOR HIGH AND LOW ACHIEVERS

High Achievers: Encourage these students to complete the Follow-up Activity. They should also help low achievers perform many of the required tasks.

Low Achievers: These students should be in a cooperative group with high achievers and be given a more active role in performing many of the tasks. They should also be asked to help the teacher demonstrate the tasks performed in the activity.

SCORING RUBRIC

Full credit should be given to students who successfully conduct the activity in a safe manner, demonstrate proficiency in recording observations, and provide accurate, complete responses to the questions. Extra credit should be awarded to students who complete the Follow-up Activity.

 **INTERNET TIE-INS**   http://www.bsu.edu/teachers/academy/gems/
http://web.wt.net/~daba/Mineral/

QUIZ   1. Why is hardness a more accurate property for identifying minerals than the mineral's color?

2. What is the approximate hardness of a mineral you can scratch with an iron nail but not with a copper penny? Explain your answer.

3. Explain how two minerals composed of the same atoms could have different hardness values.

Name _____   Date _____

How Do We Determine the Hardness of Minerals?

 BEFORE YOU BEGIN

Scientists use various properties—such as hardness, luster, color, and specific gravity—to help identify minerals. Today, we are going to examine one of these properties: hardness. For example, have you ever used talcum powder? This powder comes from the mineral talc. Do you think that talc is hard or soft? The gemstone diamond is the hardest known mineral. Because diamonds are so hard, they are used as cutting tools in industry. Hardness is determined by how easily a mineral can be scratched compared with other minerals on the **Mohs' Hardness Scale**. In this activity, you will identify a set of minerals by comparing their hardness values against known standards.

 MATERIALS

- Several numbered "unknown" mineral specimens (such as talc, feldspar, halite, gypsum, olivine, pyroxine, biotite, pyrite, quartz, calcite, hornblende, fluorite, galena)

- Tray kit containing a glass plate, copper penny, and an iron nail
- Safety goggles

 PROCEDURE

1. Obtain a set of numbered minerals and a hardness kit tray from your teacher. **Be certain to inventory all of your samples and supplies!**

2. Observe and record the color of each of your mineral samples in the appropriate place in Data Table 1 in the Data Collection and Analysis section. **Remember that white is a color; only clear minerals are considered "colorless."**

3. Observe and record the "feel" of each of your mineral samples in the appropriate place in the same Data Table 1. Does it feel smooth or rough?

4. Test the hardness of the specimens using the tools in your tray kit (the glass plate, the copper penny, and the iron nail). Record your findings as *yes* or *no* in the appropriate place in the same Data Table 1.

   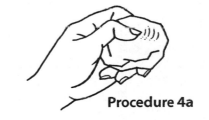
   Procedure 4a

   (a) Using your **fingernail**, try to scratch each mineral sample. If you can scratch the sample, the hardness value of the mineral is less than 2 according to the Mohs' Hardness Scale. If you cannot scratch the surface of the mineral, then the hardness value is greater than 2.

   (b) Using the **copper penny**, try to scratch each mineral sample. If you can scratch the sample, the hardness value of the mineral is less than 3 according to the Mohs' Hardness Scale. If you cannot scratch the surface of the mineral, then the hardness value is greater than 3.

   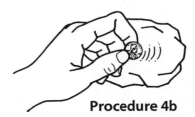
   Procedure 4b

(continued)

How Do We Determine the Hardness of Minerals? *(continued)*

(c) Using the **iron nail**, try to scratch each mineral sample. If you can scratch the sample, the hardness value of the mineral is less than 5 according to the Mohs' Hardness Scale. If you cannot scratch the surface of the mineral, then the hardness value is greater than 5.

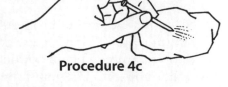

Procedure 4c

(d) Using each mineral, try to scratch the **glass plate**. If you cannot scratch the glass, the hardness value of the mineral is less than 6 according to the Mohs' Hardness Scale. If you can scratch the glass plate, then the hardness value is greater than 6.

5. Estimate the hardness value of each mineral sample, based upon the results of the various tests performed. Enter your *less than* (<) or *greater than* (>) number in the column labeled "Estimated Hardness Value" in Data Table 1.

6. Now, use the Mohs' Hardness Scale presented in Table 2 in the Data Collection and Analysis section to help identify each of your mineral samples. Record its name next to the corresponding "unknown" sample number in Data Table 3 in the Data Collection and Analysis section. Also record the reasoning behind your selection process.

Procedure 4d

DATA COLLECTION AND ANALYSIS

DATA TABLE 1: STUDENT DESCRIPTIONS AND HARDNESS-TEST RESULTS

Mineral Sample #	Color	"Feel" (Smooth or Rough)	Fingernail Test	Copper-Penny Test	Iron-Nail Test	Glass-Plate Test	Estimated Hardness Value
1							
2							
3							
4							
5							
6							
7							
8							

(continued)

How Do We Determine the Hardness of Minerals? *(continued)*

TABLE 2: MOHS' HARDNESS SCALE

Hardness	Representative Minerals	Scratch Test Performed
1	Talc	Easily scratched by fingernail
1–2	Graphite	Easily scratched by fingernail
2	Gypsum	Scratched by fingernail
2–2.5	Galena	Scratched by fingernail
2–2.5	Halite	Scratched by fingernail
2.5	Muscovite	Scratched by fingernail
2.5	Cinnabar	Scratched by fingernail
2.5–3	Biotite	Scratched by fingernail, may be scratched by a copper penny
3	Calcite	Barely scratched by copper penny
4	Fluorite	Easily scratched by iron nail
5	Apatite	Scratched by iron nail
5–6	Hornblende	Scratched by iron nail
5–6	Pyroxine	Scratched by iron nail
5.5–6	Magnetite	Barely scratched by iron nail, may scratch the glass plate
6	Feldspar	Barely scratched by iron nail, it scratches the glass plate
6–6.5	Pyrite	Barely scratched by iron nail, it scratches the glass plate
6.5–7	Olivine	May be scratched by iron nail, it scratches the glass plate
7	Quartz	It scratches iron nail and glass plate
8	Topaz	It scratches quartz
9	Corundum	It scratches topaz
10	Diamond	Hardest mineral

(continued)

How Do We Determine the Hardness of Minerals? *(continued)*

DATA TABLE 3: IDENTIFYING "UNKNOWN" MINERALS BASED UPON THEIR HARDNESS VALUES

Mineral Sample Number	Name of Mineral	Reasons for Mineral Identification
1		
2		
3		
4		
5		
6		
7		
8		

CONCLUDING QUESTIONS

1. Which can identify a mineral more accurately, its harness value or its "feel" or texture? Explain your answer. _____
   _____
   _____

2. You have two minerals, one with a hardness value of 3 and the other with a hardness value of 6. Describe the procedure for determining these hardness values. _____
   _____
   _____

3. Describe the relationship between a mineral's hardness and its ability to be worn away by the processes of weathering and erosion. _____
   _____
   _____

 **Follow-up Activity**

Research the properties and uses of each mineral studied in this activity.

How Do We Study Special Properties of Minerals?

 ## INSTRUCTIONAL OBJECTIVES

Students will be able to

- use magnetism, acid reactivity, and fluorescence tests to identify certain minerals.
- observe and compare relative properties of various minerals.
- characterize particular properties associated with certain minerals.

 ## NATIONAL SCIENCE STANDARDS ADDRESSED

Students demonstrate an understanding of

- properties of earth materials, such as rocks and minerals.
- properties and changes of properties in matter, such as chemical reactivity.
- characteristics of minerals, such as magnetism and fluorescence.
- transfer of energy, such as transformation of energy as light.

Students demonstrate scientific inquiry and problem-solving skills by

- working in teams to collect and share information and ideas.

Students demonstrate effective scientific communication by

- representing data and results in the form of tables.

Students demonstrate competence with the tools and techniques of science by

- using technology and tools, such as laboratory equipment.

 ## MATERIALS

- Several minerals (whole and crushed and placed in vials) displaying magnetic, fluorescent, and acid-reacting properties (such as magnetite, hematite, halite, pyrite, quartz, dolomite, calcite, fluorite, willemite, sphalerite)
- Tray kit containing dilute HCl, bar magnet, *alnico* magnet, clear plastic acetate sheet, 2-ounce plastic cups, several paper clips
- Eye dropper
- Safety goggles, laboratory aprons, latex gloves
- Ultraviolet (UV) long-wave light source

 = Safety icon

HELPFUL HINTS AND DISCUSSION

Time frame: One or two class periods, depending upon how many samples are tested

Structure: Cooperative learning groups of four students

Location: In science laboratory

Use mineral identification kits and fluorescent mineral kits or 2-inch square samples that can be purchased through major science supply companies. For the magnetic property test and the acid-reactivity test, you may wish to have crushed samples placed in small vials for each group to use. If this is not possible, students can try to induce a magnetic field in a large specimen by passing an *alnico* magnet in one direction close to (but not touching) the mineral; they can then determine whether the specimen can lift paper clips. This is an alternate method to test for magnetic properties in minerals.

Be certain to prepare a separate answer key for each group. If the lesson is conducted in cooperative-group format, assign each group member a particular property test to perform. **Safety procedures must be followed, particularly when using the acid and the UV-light source.** Be sure to define and explain difficult terms, such as fluorescence and orientation. Give examples of each type of luster so that the students can categorize their own samples correctly.

ADAPTATIONS FOR HIGH AND LOW ACHIEVERS

High Achievers: Encourage these students to complete the Follow-up Activity. They should also help low achievers perform many of the required tasks.

Low Achievers: These students should be in a cooperative group with high achievers and be given a more active role in performing many of the tasks. They should also be asked to help the teacher demonstrate the tasks performed in the activity.

SCORING RUBRIC

Full credit should be given to students who successfully conduct the activity in a safe manner, demonstrate proficiency in recording observations, and provide accurate, complete responses to the questions. Extra credit should be awarded to students who complete the Follow-up Activity.

**INTERNET TIE-INS**   http://www.lam.mus.ca.us/lacmnh/departments/research/mineralogy/
http://www.idahomining.org/minerals.html

QUIZ   1. How do you determine whether a mineral exhibits magnetic properties?
2. Some minerals react with acids. What does the "bubbling" represent?
3. Explain why certain minerals display fluorescence when exposed to ultraviolet light.

Name _____   Date _____

How Do We Study Special Properties of Minerals?

 BEFORE YOU BEGIN

Many minerals display special properties, including the ability to **fluoresce** (glow brightly) in ultraviolet light, to attract magnetically, and to react with acids. **Fluorescence** of minerals occurs when ultraviolet light causes the atoms making up the minerals to become excited. As the electrons in these atoms absorb the energy of the ultraviolet light, they are boosted to a higher energy level. **Magnetic attraction** occurs when the atoms within the mineral (or rock) are lined up in a way that creates a magnetic field. Some minerals contain certain molecules that react with weak acids to release carbon dioxide (CO_2). Scientists use these properties to help them identify minerals found in rocks and soil. In this investigation, you will use simple tests to identify the special properties in selected minerals.

 MATERIALS

- Several minerals (whole and crushed and placed in vials) displaying magnetic, fluorescent, and acid-reacting properties (such as magnetite, hematite, halite, pyrite, quartz, dolomite, calcite, fluorite, willemite, sphalerite)

-  Tray kit containing dilute HCl, bar magnet, *alnico* magnet, clear plastic acetate sheet, 2-ounce plastic cups, several paper clips
- Eye dropper
- Safety goggles, laboratory aprons, latex gloves
- ultraviolet (UV) long-wave light source

⊗ = Safety icon

 PROCEDURE

1. Obtain a set of minerals and tray kit from your teacher. **Be certain to inventory all of your samples and supplies!**

2. Write down the names of the minerals you are testing in this activity in Data Table 1 of the Data Collection and Analysis section.

3. Observe and record the **color** of each of your mineral samples in the appropriate place in Data Table 1. **Remember that white is a color; only clear minerals are considered colorless.**

4. Observe and record the **luster** of each of your mineral samples in the appropriate place in Data Table 1. Classify the mineral's luster as **metallic** (like polished metal), **shiny** (submetallic), **pearly** (glistening like a pearl), **vitreous** (glassy look), or **resinous** (waxy look). If you have difficulty classifying a mineral's luster, ask your teacher for help.

5. Test your specimens for **magnetic** properties by following Steps (a) through (e) below. Record your findings by writing either *yes* or *no* in the appropriate place in Data Table 1.

   (a) Place a "pinch" of each crushed sample onto the center of the clear plastic acetate sheet.

   (b) Hold the sample and sheet with one hand, and use the other hand to hold the magnet beneath the sheet directly under the sample.

(continued)

How Do We Study Special Properties of Minerals? *(continued)*

    (c) Slowly wave the magnet back and forth and watch for movement (or reorientation) of the mineral pieces.

    (d) If you see movement, then the mineral displays **magnetic** behavior. If no movement of the crushed mineral fragments occurs, then the sample is **nonmagnetic**.

    (e) Return all unused, uncontaminated samples to their appropriate vial.

6. To test your specimens for **acid-reacting** properties, follow Steps (a) through (d) below. Record your findings by writing either *yes* or *no* in the appropriate place in the Data Table 1. **Be certain to wear latex gloves, a laboratory apron, and safety goggles during acid tests. Be sure to do this under the strict supervision of your teacher or another adult.**

    (a) Place a "pinch" of each crushed sample into 2-ounce plastic cups.

    (b) Place three to five drops of dilute HCl onto the sample in each plastic cup.

    (c) If bubbling is observed, then carbon dioxide has been produced, and the mineral is **acid reactive**. If no bubbling of the crushed mineral fragments occurs, then the sample is **nonreactive** to acid.

    (d) Call your teacher to pick up the acid-containing cups for safe removal and disposal at the **end** of the lab activity.

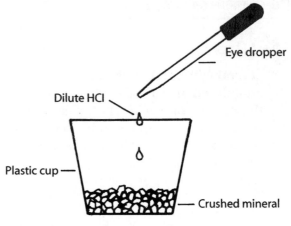

Procedure 6

7. Test your specimens for **fluorescence** by following Steps (a) through (c) below. Record your findings by writing either *yes* or *no* in the appropriate place in Data Table 1. **Perform this under the strict supervision of your teacher at the teacher's demonstration table. Wear safety goggles when using the UV-light source, and be careful not to look right at the light.**

    (a) Place your specimens (whole or crushed) on a sheet of white paper, and wait for the teacher to call your group to bring them to the demonstration table.

    (b) Your teacher will irradiate the specimens with the UV light.

    (c) If the sample glows, then the mineral is **fluorescent**. If the mineral specimen does not glow, then the sample is **nonfluorescent**. **Observing any color other than that of the UV-light source itself is considered evidence of fluorescence.**

(continued)

Name _____   Date _____

 DATA COLLECTION AND ANALYSIS

DATA TABLE 1: STUDENT RESULTS OF TESTS FOR SPECIAL MINERAL PROPERTIES

Mineral Sample	Color	Luster	Magnetism	Acid Reactivity	Fluorescence

CONCLUDING QUESTIONS

1. Which of your samples possessed **magnetic** properties? Describe any relationship between the color, luster, and magnetic properties of those minerals. _____

_____

_____

_____

2. Identify the minerals that tested positive to the **acid reactivity** test. Which one(s) would you describe as showing the highest reactivity? _____

_____

_____

3. Which of your mineral specimens exhibited **fluorescence**? Explain how this property is different from the color of the mineral. _____

_____

_____

_____

(continued)

Follow-up Activity

Prepare a *Mineral Identification Chart* game board like the example below. Color code 3-inch by 5-inch index cards in two distinct colors (for example, blue and yellow). List the minerals examined in this activity. Under each mineral name, place a blue card for *positive* results or a yellow card for *negative* results for each property test. Your class can now build a more visual "database" for minerals studied. You can also include previously studied minerals and the other tests used for mineral identification.

MINERAL IDENTIFICATION CHART

Properties	Mineral X	Mineral Y	Mineral Z
Magnetism	Yellow Card (No)	Blue Card (Yes)	Yellow Card (No)
Fluorescence	Blue Card (Yes)	Yellow Card (No)	Yellow Card (No)
Acid Reactivity	Blue Card (Yes)	Yellow Card (No)	Yellow Card (No)
Hardness	4	7	2
Luster	Nonmetallic	Metallic	Nonmetallic
Etc.			

How Do We Identify "Unknown" Minerals?

 INSTRUCTIONAL OBJECTIVES

Students will be able to

- use hardness, streak, magnetism, acid reactivity, and fluorescence tests to identify certain minerals.
- observe and compare relative properties of various minerals.
- identify an "unknown" mineral through testing methods.

 NATIONAL SCIENCE STANDARDS ADDRESSED

Students demonstrate an understanding of

- properties of earth materials, such as rocks and minerals.
- properties and changes of properties in matter, such as chemical reactivity.
- characteristics of minerals, such as hardness, streak, magnetism, and fluorescence.
- transfer of energy, such as transformation of energy as light.

Students demonstrate scientific inquiry and problem-solving skills by

- working individually and in teams to collect and share information and ideas.
- classifying the outcome of an investigation by determining the identity of an "unknown" mineral.

Students demonstrate effective scientific communication by

- representing data and results in the form of tables.

 MATERIALS

- Numbered "unknown" mineral specimens (whole or crushed and placed in vials)
- Tray kit containing dilute HCl, bar magnet, *alnico* magnet, a glass plate, a copper penny, an iron nail, a streak plate, clear plastic acetate sheet, 2-ounce plastic cups, several paper clips
- Safety goggles, laboratory aprons, latex gloves
- Ultraviolet (UV) long-wave light source

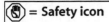 = Safety icon

HELPFUL HINTS AND DISCUSSION

Time frame: Two class periods
Structure: Cooperative learning groups of four students
Location: In the classroom or in science laboratory

Before doing this activity, students must have completed two previous activities in this manual: "How Do We Determine the Hardness of Minerals?" and "How Do We Study Special Properties of Minerals?" These other activities build necessary skills and provide preliminary procedures for the various mineral tests that the students will employ for this activity.

Use mineral identification kits and fluorescent mineral kits or 2-inch square samples that can be purchased through major science supply companies. For the magnetic property test and the acid-reactivity test, you may wish to have crushed samples placed in small vials for each group to use. If this is not possible, students can try to induce a magnetic field in a large specimen by passing an *alnico* magnet in one direction close to (but not touching) the mineral; they can then determine whether the specimen can lift paper clips. This is an alternate method to test for magnetic properties in minerals.

For this "unknown" identification activity, randomly number the specimens and distribute a variety of samples to each student group. Only when the students have completed all the property-test tasks should you distribute Data Table 4: Mineral Identifier Data for them to identify their particular samples. If the lesson is conducted in a cooperative-group format, assign each group member a particular property test to perform.

Safety procedures must be followed, particularly when using the acid, the UV-light source, the streak plate, the iron nail, and the glass plate.

ADAPTATIONS FOR HIGH AND LOW ACHIEVERS

High Achievers: Encourage these students to complete the Follow-up Activity. They should also help low achievers perform many of the required tasks.

Low Achievers: These students should be in a cooperative group with high achievers and be given a more active role in performing many of the tasks. They should also be asked to help the teacher demonstrate the tasks performed in the activity.

SCORING RUBRIC

Full credit should be given to students who successfully conduct the activity in a safe manner, demonstrate proficiency in recording observations, and provide accurate, complete responses to the questions. Extra credit should be awarded to students who complete the Follow-up Activity.

 INTERNET TIE-INS   http://www.lam.mus.ca.us/lacmnh/departments/research/mineralogy/
http://www.bsu.edu/teachers/academy/gems/galleries.html
http://web.wt.net/~daba/Mineral/

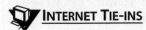 **QUIZ**   1. Explain the importance of performing several property tests to help identify a mineral.
2. Distinguish between *fluorescence* of a mineral and *reflection of light* by a mineral.
3. How does the property of streak color differ from the actual color of a mineral sample?
4. State two safety procedures that you followed when performing mineral property tests.

Name _____ Date _____

 BEFORE YOU BEGIN

You may have seen interesting rock samples in a museum or in the field. These samples possess minerals with unique properties, characteristic of only that type of mineral. Scientists use simple tests for physical and chemical characteristics to help them identify minerals. For example, testing a mineral's hardness and its ability to fluoresce when exposed to particular wavelengths of ultraviolet light helps identify that mineral. The streak color it may leave when rubbed against an **unglazed** porcelain or ceramic plate is another such test. Also, the ability of the specimen to produce a magnetic field and its reactivity to weak acids are other tests used to help in the mineral's identification. In this investigation, you will use a variety of tests to identify "unknown" specimens.

 **MATERIALS**

- Numbered "unknown" mineral specimens (whole or crushed and placed in vials)
- Tray kit containing dilute HCl, bar magnet, *alnico* magnet, a glass plate, a copper penny, an iron nail, a streak plate, clear plastic acetate sheet, 2-ounce plastic cups, several paper clips

- Safety goggles, laboratory aprons, latex gloves
-  Ultraviolet (UV) long-wave light source

 = Safety icon

PROCEDURE: HARDNESS TEST

1. Obtain a set of numbered "unknown" minerals and a tray kit from your teacher. **Be certain to inventory all of your samples and supplies!**

2. Test the **hardness** of your specimens using the tools in your tray kit (the glass plate, the copper penny, and the iron nail). Record your findings as *yes* or *no* in the appropriate place in Data Table 1 in the Data Collection and Analysis section.

   (a) Try to scratch each mineral sample with your **fingernail**. If you can scratch the sample, the hardness value of the mineral is less than 2 according to the Mohs' Hardness Scale. If you cannot scratch the surface of the mineral, then the hardness value is greater than 2.

   (b) Using the **copper penny**, try to scratch each mineral sample. If you can scratch the sample, the hardness value of the mineral is less than 3 according to the Mohs' Hardness Scale. If you cannot scratch the surface of the mineral, then the hardness value is greater than 3.

   (c) Try to scratch each mineral sample with the **iron nail**. If you can scratch the sample, the hardness value of the mineral is less than 5 according to the Mohs' Hardness Scale. If you cannot scratch the surface of the mineral, then the hardness value is greater than 5.

   (d) Using each mineral, try to scratch the **glass plate**. If you cannot scratch the glass, the hardness value of the mineral is less than 6 according to the Mohs' Hardness Scale. If you can scratch the glass plate, then the hardness value is greater than 6.

(continued)

How Do We Identify "Unknown" Minerals? *(continued)*

3. Estimate the hardness of each mineral sample, based on the results of your various tests. Enter your *less than* (<) or *greater than* (>) number in the last column in Data Table 1 in the Data Collection and Analysis section.

4. Transfer your estimated hardness data for each "unknown" mineral from Data Table 1 to the "Hardness" column of Data Table 2 in the Data Collection and Analysis section.

 ## PROCEDURE: COLOR, LUSTER, AND STREAK TEST

1. Observe and record the **color** of each of your mineral samples in the appropriate place in Data Table 2 in the Data Collection and Analysis section. **Remember that white is a color; only clear minerals are considered "colorless."**

2. Observe and record the **luster** of each of your mineral samples in the appropriate place in Data Table 2. Classify the mineral's luster as **metallic** (like polished metal), **shiny** (submetallic), **pearly** (glistening like a pearl), **vitreous** (glassy look), or **resinous** (waxy look). If you are having difficulty classifying a mineral's luster, ask your teacher for help.

3. Place the streak plate flat on the table and rub your mineral sample across the surface of the streak plate.

4. Examine the trail of powder that may be left on the streak plate, if the mineral is softer than the streak plate.

5. If the powder has a color, record the **streak color** in Data Table 2 in the Data Collection and Analysis section.

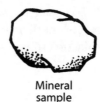

Mineral sample

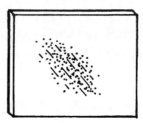

Streak plate

6. If the mineral is harder than the streak plate, there will be no streak color. Record "no streak" in Data Table 2.

PROCEDURE: MAGNETIC PROPERTIES

1. Test your specimens for magnetic properties and record your findings in the appropriate place in Data Table 2.

   (a) Place a pinch of each crushed sample onto the center of the clear plastic acetate sheet.

   (b) Hold the sample and sheet with one hand, and with the other hand, hold the magnet beneath the sheet directly under the sample.

   (c) Slowly wave the magnet back and forth, and watch for movement (or reorientation) of the mineral pieces.

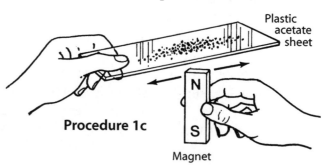

Plastic acetate sheet

Procedure 1c

Magnet

(continued)

How Do We Identify "Unknown" Minerals? *(continued)*

(d) If you see movement, then the mineral displays **magnetic** behavior. If no movement of the crushed mineral fragments occurs, then the sample is **nonmagnetic**.

(e) Return all unused, uncontaminated samples to their appropriate vial.

 PROCEDURE: ACID REACTIVITY

1. Test your specimens for **acid-reacting** properties and record your findings by writing *yes* or *no* in the appropriate place in the data table. Ⓝ **Students should wear latex gloves, a laboratory apron, and safety goggles during acid tests. Be sure to do this under the strict supervision of your teacher.**

    (a) Place a pinch of each crushed sample into 2-ounce plastic cups.

    (b) Place three to five drops of dilute HCl onto the sample in each plastic cup.

    (c) If you see bubbling, then the mineral is **acid reactive**. If no bubbling of the crushed mineral fragments occurs, then the sample is **nonreactive** to acid.

    (d) At the end of the lab activity, call your teacher to pick up the acid-containing cups for safe removal and disposal.

 PROCEDURE: FLUORESCENCE TEST

1. Test your specimens for **fluorescence** and record your findings by writing *yes* or *no* in the appropriate place in the data table. Ⓝ **This test will be performed at the teacher's demonstration table. Wear safety goggles when using the UV-light source, and be careful not to look right at the light.**

    (a) Place your specimens (whole or crushed) on a sheet of white paper, and wait for your teacher to call your group to bring them to the demonstration table.

    (b) Your teacher will irradiate the specimens with the UV light.

    (c) If the sample glows, then the mineral is **fluorescent**. If it does not glow, then the sample is **nonfluorescent. Observing any color other than that of the UV-light source itself is considered evidence of fluorescence.**

 PROCEDURE: MINERAL IDENTIFICATION

1. Once you have completed all of the above tests, ask your teacher for Data Table 4: Mineral Identifier Data, which provides a list of common minerals and their properties.

2. Examine your data for each of the properties tested, and compare this with the properties on Data Table 4 to determine the identity of your "unknown" samples.

3. Identify each of your "unknown" specimens by name in Data Table 3 in the Data Collection and Analysis section.

4. Provide supporting evidence for each of your selections in the "Reasons" column in Data Table 3.

(continued)

Name _____ Date _____

DATA COLLECTION AND ANALYSIS

DATA TABLE 1: STUDENT HARDNESS-TEST RESULTS

Mineral Sample #	Fingernail Test	Copper-Penny Test	Iron-Nail Test	Glass-Plate Test	Estimated Hardness Value
1					
2					
3					
4					

DATA TABLE 2: TESTING "UNKNOWN" MINERALS

Mineral Sample #	Hardness	Color	Luster	Streak Color	Magnetism	Acid Reactivity	Fluorescence
1							
2							
3							
4							

(continued)

How Do We Identify "Unknown" Minerals? *(continued)*

DATA TABLE 3: IDENTIFYING "UNKNOWN" MINERALS

Mineral Sample No.	Name of Mineral	Reasons for Mineral Identification
1		
2		
3		
4		

CONCLUDING QUESTIONS

1. Which of your minerals had a color different from its streak color? What was the color of the mineral, and what was the color of the streak? _____
_____

2. Explain one reason why your observations for each of your identified minerals may not have exactly matched the data information in Data Table 4: Mineral Identifier Data. _____
_____
_____
_____
_____

3. Which mineral property did you find the most difficult to determine? Explain your answer.
_____
_____
_____

Follow-up Activity

The **specific gravity** of a mineral can easily be determined by comparing the weight of a mineral in air to the weight of an equal volume of water. This ratio indicates how many times more dense the mineral is than water. Study the data for specific gravity listed in Data Table 4: Mineral Identifier Data. Select minerals with a specific gravity value from 4.8 to 5.2. List those minerals with their corresponding hardness, luster, magnetism, acid-reactivity, and fluorescence characteristics. Group them according to similarities of these characteristics. Identify which characteristic is very closely correlated to the specific gravity value. Explain your findings.

(continued)

How Do We Identify "Unknown" Minerals? *(continued)*

DATA TABLE 4: MINERAL IDENTIFIER DATA

Mineral	Hardness	Color	Luster	Streak	Magnetism	Acid Reactivity	Fluorescence	Specific Gravity
Apatite	5.0	Greenish-white, brown, yellow	Vitreous, resinous	White	No	No	No	3.2–3.4
Biotite	2.4–3.1	Black, greenish-black	Shiny	White	No	No	No	2.6–3.0
Calcite	3.0	Colorless, white	Shiny	No color	No	Yes	No	2.7
Dolomite	3.5–4.0	White, reddish-brown, greenish	Pearly	Same as color	No	Yes	No	3.0
Fluorite	4.0	Yellowish, bluish, colorless	Vitreous	White	No	Yes	Yes	3.0–3.3
Galena	2.5–2.8	Gray	Metallic	Gray	No	No	No	4.7–4.8
Gypsum	1.5–2.0	White, pale gray	Pearly	White	No	Yes	No	2.3
Halite	2.5	Colorless, white	Vitreous	Same as color	No	No	No	2.1–2.6
Hematite	5.5–6.5	Gray, earthy red	Metallic	Red	Yes	Yes	No	4.9–5.3
Hornblende	5.0–6.0	Black, greenish-black	Vitreous	No color	Yes	No	No	3.0–3.5
Magnetite	5.5–6.5	Black	Metallic	Black	Yes	No	No	5.2
Muscovite	2.5–3.0	Colorless, pale brown	Vitreous, pearly	No color	No	No	No	2.7–3.0
Pyrite	6.0–6.5	Brassy gold	Metallic	Greenish-black	Yes	No	No	4.9–5.0
Quartz	7.0	Colorless, white, yellow	Vitreous	Same as color	No	No	Yes	2.6–2.7
Sphalerite	3.5–4.0	Yellow-brown green-white	Resinous	Brownish-yellow	No	No	Yes	3.9–4.1

How Do Different Ways of Cooling Form Different Types of Rocks?

TEACHER RESOURCE PAGE

 INSTRUCTIONAL OBJECTIVES

Students will be able to

- describe features found in an igneous rock that indicate its rate of cooling.
- identify the different types of magma (felsic or mafic) that can form igneous rocks.
- classify igneous rocks according to physical properties.

 NATIONAL SCIENCE STANDARDS ADDRESSED

Students demonstrate an understanding of

- structure of the earth system, such as rock cycles.
- big ideas and unifying concepts, such as order and organization.

Students demonstrate effective scientific communication by

- representing data in multiple ways, including tables.

 MATERIALS

- Pen/pencil
- Several igneous rock samples (basalt, andesite, rhyolite, gabbro, diorite, granite, obsidian, scoria, tuff, and pumice)
- Magnifying glass

HELPFUL HINTS AND DISCUSSION

Time frame: One class period
Structure: Individuals or cooperative learning groups of three students
Location: In class

In this activity students will observe several different igneous rocks and determine how certain physical properties, such as rate of cooling and type of magma, caused them to cool as they did.

You may choose to have either enough small samples for each student group or a few larger samples that students can share. Larger samples do make it easier for students to see differences in crystal sizes. This activity should be performed after students have studied the formation of igneous rocks. The rock samples should be labeled alphabetically from *A* to *I* to assist student record keeping.

ADAPTATIONS FOR HIGH AND LOW ACHIEVERS

High Achievers: Encourage these students to determine the actual mineral makeup of the igneous rocks by identifying the individual crystals found in some rocks. Have them create a report and present it to the class.

Low Achievers: These students may need an adult's or teacher's help in using the flowchart to identify the samples.

SCORING RUBRIC

Full credit should be given to students who correctly identify and classify the different samples and answer all the questions successfully.

 **INTERNET TIE-INS**
http://www.wsu.edu:8080/~geology/geol101/igneous/igneous.htm
http://volcano.und.nodak.edu/
http://www.halcyon.com/rdpayne/mshnvm.html

 QUIZ
1. How do mafic magmas differ from felsic magmas?
2. How is the crystal size of an igneous rock related to its place of formation?
3. Rocks that form from mafic magmas are usually dense; however, scoria is a relatively light mafic rock. How can you explain this?

How Do Different Ways of Cooling Form Different Types of Rocks?

▨ BEFORE YOU BEGIN ▨

You may have seen pictures of volcanoes streaming with molten rock (lava). **Lava**, which is called **magma** before it reaches the surface, is composed of extremely hot minerals. All rocks that begin as magma are classified as **igneous rocks** once they cool and become solid.

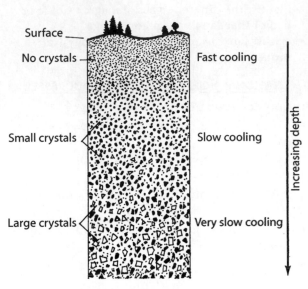

Crystal size and cooling rate

The cooling rate of magma determines the size of the mineral crystals in the rock. When lava cools (and solidifies) very quickly, the mineral crystals do not have much time to form. We call these rocks **volcanic**, and you can identify them by their small or imperceptible crystals. Many times, these rocks cool so fast that pockets of air are trapped inside. These rocks appear to contain air holes and are usually light in weight. These rocks are called **frothy**. Other volcanic rocks cool so quickly that they form a clear, glasslike surface with no apparent crystals. These rocks are called **glassy**.

When magma cools deep underground, the process is slower, and the resulting **mineral crystals** have time to become large enough to see with the naked eye. These rocks are known as **plutonic**.

Another influence on the appearance of igneous rocks is the mineral composition of the magma. **Felsic** magmas are high in feldspars (aluminum silicates) and are usually **light** colored with low densities. Other magmas high in iron and magnesium are known as **mafic**. They tend to be dark colored with high densities. Some grayish igneous rocks are a combination of the different types of magma. These rocks can be classified as **intermediate**. The large amount of Plagioclase feldspar they contain gives these igneous rocks their grayish color.

In this activity, you will observe several different mineral samples. Based on the properties of these samples, you will determine where they formed and what minerals they contain.

✂ MATERIALS

- Magnifying glass
- Several igneous rock samples (basalt, andesite, rhyolite, gabbro, diorite, granite, obsidian, scoria, tuff, and pumice)

- Pen/pencil

(continued)

How Do Different Ways of Cooling Form Different Types of Rocks?
(continued)

Various sizes of crystals in rocks

 PROCEDURE

1. You will work in groups of three students. One member will record all the observations, another member will obtain samples from the teacher, and the third member will examine the rock specimens and lead the group in describing them.

2. When the group receives a sample, the observer will examine it carefully. The observer will then share the following information with the group, and the recorder will enter it into the "Observation of Sample" column of Data Table 1:

   (a) Color

   (b) Texture (feel)

   (c) Density (light or heavy)

   (d) Crystal size

3. Now, based on the crystal size of the sample, determine whether or not your igneous rock is plutonic or volcanic in origin. Record this answer in the appropriate column in Data Table 1. *Note:* You should use the magnifying glasses if you need them.

4. Determine the mineral composition of the magma from which this sample came. Use the color of the sample to decide if it was formed from mafic or felsic magma. Grayish samples should be classified as coming from **intermediate** magmas. Pink or reddish samples should be considered light in color. Record your samples as mafic, felsic, or intermediate in the appropriate column in Data Table 1.

5. Use the flowchart in Figure 1 to identify the rock sample. Place the *most likely* name of the rock sample in the space provided in Data Table 1.

(continued)

Name _____ Date _____

 DATA COLLECTION AND ANALYSIS

TABLE 1: SELECTED CHARACTERISTICS OF IGNEOUS ROCK SAMPLES

Rock Sample	Observation of Sample	Location of Formation (Volcanic or Plutonic)	Type of Magma (Mafic or Felsic)	Name of Rock
A				
B				
C				
D				
E				
F				
G				
H				
I				

(continued)

How Do Different Ways of Cooling Form Different Types of Rocks?
(continued)

FIGURE 1: FLOWCHART OF IGNEOUS ROCK IDENTIFICATION

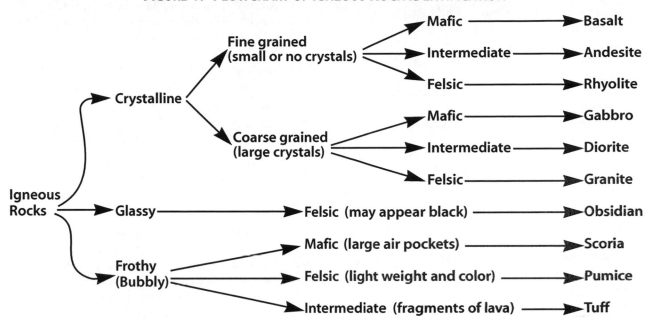

 CONCLUDING QUESTIONS

1. Why are fossilized remains not usually found in igneous rocks? _____
   _____

2. Some igneous rocks have special properties that allow them to be identified easily. Describe at least three of your samples that can be identified by a special property. _____
   _____
   _____

3. How does the formation of crystalline rocks differ from the formation of glassy rocks? _____
   _____
   _____

Follow-up Activities

1. Determine which igneous rock is commonly used as a building material. Create a report that explains what special property of this igneous rock is important in construction. Bring in samples of different materials for the class to view.

2. Take a trip to a store that specializes in kitchen and bathroom materials. Create a report on the use of granite in home furnishings. Bring in samples of materials for the class to view.

How Can We Determine the Weathering Rate of Rocks and Minerals?

INSTRUCTIONAL OBJECTIVES

Students will be able to

- identify granite, limestone, and calcite.
- demonstrate the processes of physical and chemical weathering.
- measure and graph the weathering rates of various rocks and minerals.
- prepare a solution of dissolved minerals for identification.
- examine and describe mineral crystals.

NATIONAL SCIENCE STANDARDS ADDRESSED

Students demonstrate an understanding of

- properties of earth materials, such as rocks and minerals.
- geochemical cycles, such as conversion of matter.
- Earth's history, such as earth processes including erosion and rock cycles.

Students demonstrate scientific inquiry and problem-solving skills by

- working individually and in teams to collect and share information and ideas.
- using evidence from reliable sources to develop explanations.

Students demonstrate effective scientific communication by

- representing data and results in the form of tables and graphs.

Students demonstrate competence with the tools and techniques of science by

- using technology and tools, such as laboratory equipment.

MATERIALS

- Picture of the Grand Canyon
- Granite, limestone, and calcite specimens (chips)
- Tray kit containing a hand lens, dilute HCl, filter paper, weighing paper, matches or striker, 2-ounce plastic cups, grease pencil, colored pencils
- 100-ml graduated cylinders
- Three 250-ml beakers
- Three watch glasses or three evaporating dishes
- Ring stand, ring, and wire gauze
- Bunsen burner
- Three 250-ml polyethylene plastic bottles
- 4-inch square fine wire mesh (or screen wire)
- Triple beam balance scale
- Paper towels
- Safety goggles, laboratory aprons, latex gloves
- Stopwatch (optional)

 = Safety icon

HELPFUL HINTS AND DISCUSSION

Time frame: Two class periods
Structure: Cooperative learning groups of four students
Location: In a science laboratory

Prepare small fragment-sized pieces of granite (igneous rock), limestone (sedimentary rock), and calcite (mineral salt). Larger 2-inch square samples can be purchased through major science supply companies. To prepare fragment-sized pieces, place the larger specimens inside of a piece of cloth, and carefully hammer each rock or mineral until you achieve the desired size. It will not take that much effort to produce fragment-sized pieces of calcite. The chips should be roughly uniform in size. You should separate out the pieces appropriately sized for this activity. Pre-soak the granite and limestone chips for at least two hours (or, preferably, overnight) before you begin the activity. You should demonstrate how to use a triple-beam balance properly prior to this activity, and students should be proficient in its use.

Be certain to prepare a model answer key for an approximate weathering rate for each specimen and for the dissolved mineral samples. Granite and limestone should be much more resistant to the weathering process. Upon examination, soluble calcite should exhibit a rhomboid shape. If the lesson is conducted in cooperative-group format, assign each group member a rock or mineral to prepare for each section of the exercise. Only clean glassware and distilled water should be used when preparing the samples for soluble minerals.

 Safety procedures must be followed, particularly when using the acid, alcohol lamp, and the matches (or striker).

ADAPTATIONS FOR HIGH AND LOW ACHIEVERS

High Achievers: These students should be encouraged to complete the Follow-up Activity. They should also help low achievers perform many of the required tasks.

Low Achievers: These students should be in a cooperative group with high achievers and be given a more active role in performing many of the tasks. They should also be asked to help the teacher demonstrate the tasks performed in the activity.

SCORING RUBRIC

Full credit should be given to students who successfully conduct the activity in a safe manner, demonstrate proficiency in recording observations, and provide accurate, complete responses to the questions. Extra credit should be awarded to students who complete the Follow-up Activity.

 **INTERNET TIE-INS**   http://www.kdu.com/caveform.html
http://www.goodearthgraphics.com/virtcave.html

 QUIZ   1. Distinguish between *chemical* and *physical* weathering processes.
2. Which rock type experiences the least amount of weathering? The greatest amount of weathering?
3. Why do different rock types weather at different rates?
4. Describe the environmental factors that most influence the weathering of rocks.

How Can We Determine the Weathering Rate of Rocks and Minerals?

 BEFORE YOU BEGIN

Look at a picture of the Grand Canyon and try to imagine how it was formed. Most of it was shaped by physical and chemical weathering and erosion. Chemical weathering takes place when a rock's reaction to chemicals causes the rock material to change. For example, acids in the environment react chemically with rocks, causing them to break down. Physical weathering results from a rock's contact with such materials as water, wind, ice and other rocks. This physical contact can change the size and/or shape of the original rock. Erosion happens when wind and/or water move the weathered material from its original site.

While you were looking at the picture of the Grand Canyon, you may have noticed that some areas are more weathered than others. What determines the weathering rate of rock materials? The rate of chemical weathering is based on several properties. These include the climate and the way the rock reacts to chemicals in rain and gases in the atmosphere, such as carbon dioxide. The speed of weathering is determined by how resistant the rock is to these processes. Several factors influence this resistance. They include the amount of surface exposed, the minerals in the rock, and the additional damage caused by the weathered particles rubbing against the rock. Keep in mind that weathering takes millions of years to form canyons and caverns. Scientists study the effects of weathering to explain a variety of natural rock formations that beautify our Earth.

In this activity, you will measure and graph the rate at which sample rocks weather, and their acid reactivity. You will also identify the mineral composition of any material dissolved from your sample rocks or minerals.

 MATERIALS

- Picture of the Grand Canyon
- Granite, limestone, and calcite specimens (chips)
- Tray kit containing a hand lens, dilute HCl, filter paper, weighing paper, matches or striker, 2-ounce plastic cups, grease pencil, colored pencils
- 100-ml graduated cylinders
- Three 250-ml beakers
- Three watch glasses or three evaporating dishes
- Ring stand, ring, and wire gauze

-  Bunsen burner
- Three 250-ml polyethylene plastic bottles
- 4-inch square fine wire mesh (or screen wire)
- Triple beam balance scale
- Paper towels
- Safety goggles, laboratory aprons, latex gloves
- Stopwatch (optional)

 = Safety icon

 PROCEDURE: SECTION A

1. Obtain granite, limestone, and calcite chips from your teacher.

(continued)

How Can We Determine the Weathering Rate of Rocks and Minerals?
(continued)

2. Observe and record the appearance of each of your samples in the appropriate place in Data Table 1 of the Data Collection and Analysis section. Use your hand lens to describe any such characteristics as particles, crystal shapes, and colors that you detect.

3. Test your specimens for acid-reacting properties by doing the following:
     Be sure to do this under the strict supervision of your teacher. Wear latex gloves, a laboratory apron, and safety goggles during the acid tests.
    (a) Place five granite chips into a 2-ounce plastic cup.
    (b) Place three to five drops of dilute HCl onto the sample in the plastic cup.
    (c) If bubbling is observed, then the mineral is **acid reactive**. If no bubbling of the crushed mineral chips occurs, then the sample is **nonreactive** to acid.
    (d) Record your findings in Data Table 1.
    (e) Repeat the procedure outlined in Steps 3(a) through 3(d), using the limestone chips.
    (f) Repeat, using the calcite chips.
    (g) At the end of the lab activity, call your teacher to pick up the acid-containing cups for safe removal and disposal.

PROCEDURE: SECTION B

1. Review how to use the triple beam balance with your teacher. Then use this scale to measure out 30 grams of each sample. Be certain to subtract the mass of the weighing paper. Record this data as the zero-minute time value in Data Table 2 of the Data Collection and Analysis section.

2. Label three plastic bottles and three 250-ml beakers, one for each of the samples studied in this activity.

3. Place the rock/mineral chips into their respective plastic bottles. Measure out and add 100-ml of distilled water to each bottle.

4. Screw the cap onto each bottle and shake at a slow, steady, rate for two minutes.

5. Unscrew the cap, place a fine wire mesh (or screen wire) over the mouth of the bottle, and pour out the liquid (**slurry**) into prelabeled 250-ml beakers, one for each specimen. *You need to save the liquid slurry from each sample to use during the rest of this exercise and during* **Section C** *of this laboratory activity.*

6. Remove the chips from each container, and pat dry each sample with a paper towel.

7. Use the triple beam balance to determine the mass of chips from each sample, and record the data as the two-minute time value in Data Table 2.

8. Put the samples back into their respective plastic bottles and add to each the matching liquid slurry from the 250-ml beakers.

250-ml plastic bottle

Distilled water

Rock/mineral chips

Procedures 2–3

(continued)

How Can We Determine the Weathering Rate of Rocks and Minerals?
(continued)

9. Repeat steps 3 through 7 above at two-minute intervals to obtain data for four minutes, six minutes, and eight minutes. **Be certain to add back the correct slurry mixture to the plastic bottle containing its respective sample rock or mineral.**

10. Calculate the percent of mass remaining for each sample at each time interval using the equation below:

$$\text{percent of mass remaining} = \frac{\text{mass at each time interval}}{\text{original mass of the sample}} \times 100$$

Place your results for the calculated percent of mass remaining for each sample in the appropriate spaces in Data Table 2.

11. Label the *x*- and *y*-axes and then plot your data using the line graph in Figure 1 of the Data Collection and Analysis section. Each rock or mineral will have its own set of points for each time interval (zero minutes through eight minutes). Place the time (**in minutes**) on the *x*-axis, and the percent of mass remaining on the *y*-axis. Use three different colored pencils, one to draw the graph for each rock or mineral. Enter the points for each mineral and then draw a line to connect each point.

 ### PROCEDURE: SECTION C

1. Gently swirl each slurry sample (**in the beakers**) left over from Section B to uniformly mix any sediments that may have settled on the bottom. Pour enough of each liquid solution to fill each prelabeled watch glass or evaporating dish.

2. Place each watch glass or evaporating dish on the ring stand.

3. ✋ **Under the strict supervision of your teacher, carefully light a bunsen burner, and gently warm the solution to evaporate the water completely.**

4. Allow what remains in each watch glass to cool down completely before moving to the next step.

5. Using a hand lens, examine each sample for dissolved minerals. Record your results in Data Table 3 of the Data Collection and Analysis section. Sketch any soluble mineral types you observe, and detail any observed particular geometric shapes.

 ### DATA COLLECTION AND ANALYSIS

DATA TABLE 1: STUDENT RESULTS TO DESCRIBE PROPERTIES OF ROCK AND MINERAL SAMPLES

Sample	Appearance of Specimens	Reacts with Acid (Yes or No)
Granite		
Limestone		
Calcite		

(continued)

How Can We Determine the Weathering Rate of Rocks and Minerals?
(continued)

DATA TABLE 2: STUDENT RESULTS TO MEASURE THE WEATHERING RATE OF ROCK AND MINERAL SAMPLES

Mass and Percentage (%) Remaining of Rock and Mineral Samples						
Time (Minutes)	Granite (Mass)	(%)	Limestone (Mass)	(%)	Calcite (Mass)	(%)
0						
2						
4						
6						
8						

FIGURE 1: WEATHERING RATE OF ROCK AND MINERAL SAMPLES

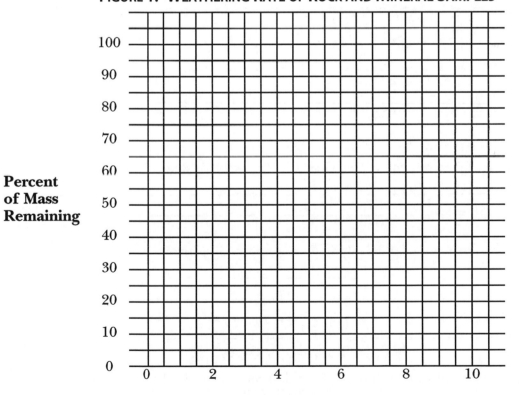

Percent of Mass Remaining

Time (in Minutes)

(continued)

How Can We Determine the Weathering Rate of Rocks and Minerals?
(continued)

DATA TABLE 3: STUDENT DESCRIPTIONS OF SOLUBLE MINERALS IN ROCK AND MINERAL SAMPLES

Sample	Visual Characteristics of Solute Minerals	Sketches
Granite		
Limestone		
Calcite		

CONCLUDING QUESTIONS

1. Did certain rocks or minerals weather at a slower rate than others? Why do you think this happened? _____
_____

2. Identify which materials displayed a chemical weathering process, and explain why this is chemical weathering. _____
_____
_____

3. Why did you add the same "slurry" mixture back to each sample bottle each time? How would your results have differed if you added clean distilled water instead? _____
_____
_____

4. Describe the various types of physical weathering that took place in this activity. _____
_____
_____

 **Follow-up Activity**

Research how canyons form and write a detailed report on their development.

How Do Erosion, Deposition, and Cementation Form Rocks?

 INSTRUCTIONAL OBJECTIVES

Students will be able to
- describe features found in sedimentary rocks.
- explain how the processes of erosion, deposition, and cementation form sedimentary rock.
- classify sedimentary rocks according to the constituent materials.

 NATIONAL SCIENCE STANDARDS ADDRESSED

Students demonstrate an understanding of
- structure of the earth system, such as rock cycles.
- big ideas and unifying concepts, such as order and organization.

Students demonstrate effective scientific communication by
- representing data in multiple ways, including tables.

 MATERIALS

- Pen/pencil
- Several sedimentary rock samples (coquina, fossil limestone, breccia, conglomerate, sandstone, shale, chalk, rock gypsum, rock salt, limestone, and bituminous coal)
- Magnifying glass

HELPFUL HINTS AND DISCUSSION

Time frame: One class period
Structure: Individuals or cooperative learning groups of three students
Location: In class

In this activity, students will observe and identify several different sedimentary rocks as clastic, chemical, or organic, using Figure 1. Based on this identification and the information found in the Before You Begin section, they will relate how these rocks were created.

You may choose to have either enough small samples for each student group or a few larger samples that students can share. Larger samples do make it easier for students to see differences. This activity should be performed after students have studied the formation of sedimentary rocks. The rock samples should be labeled alphabetically from A to K to assist student record keeping.

ADAPTATIONS FOR HIGH AND LOW ACHIEVERS

High Achievers: Encourage these students to determine what type of environment must have existed for the formation of each sedimentary rock.

Low Achievers: These students may need an adult's or teacher's help in using the flowchart to identify the samples.

SCORING RUBRIC

Full credit should be given to students who correctly identify and classify the different samples and answer all analysis questions successfully.

 **INTERNET TIE-INS**
http://scienceweb.dao.nrc.ca/burgess/geology/cycle6.html
http://www.kgs.ukans.edu/Publications/primer/primer07.html
http://www.dnr.state.oh.us/odnr/geo_survey/edu/hands03.htm

 QUIZ
1. Why are sedimentary rocks usually an excellent source of fossilized plants and/or animals?
2. What does the existence of limestone tell us about the environment in which it formed?
3. What events must have occurred for bituminous coal to have formed?

How Do Erosion, Deposition, and Cementation Form Rocks?

  BEFORE YOU BEGIN

Types of Sedimentary Rocks

We know that dinosaurs existed because we have found their fossilized bones. **Fossils** are remains or imprints of past organisms. Fossils are usually found in a type of layered rock called **sedimentary**. When an animal or plant dies, it is sometimes covered by layers of mud, sand, or silt. Over a long period of time, these layers of material build up and harden into rocks holding the imprint or remains of the dead organism.

Sedimentary rocks can form in three ways. Exposed rocks **weather**—that is, they begin to break down into smaller pieces called **sediments**. These sediments can be carried by a stream or river until they reach the ocean. At the ocean the larger sediments will settle to the bottom first (because of gravity), while the smallest particles settle out last. After a period of time and under the right conditions, these particles may become cemented together. This process results in the formation of a rock composed of particles that are mostly the same size. These rocks are known as **clastic** sedimentary rocks. Most clastic sedimentary rocks are classified by the size of the uniform particles that make them up.

Another type of sedimentary rock is known as **chemical** sedimentary rock. It is formed when a lake evaporates and only the solid minerals (salt, calcite) that were dissolved in the water are left. These minerals can now build up and solidify into rocks. Limestone is an example of a chemical sedimentary rock. It is composed almost entirely of calcite.

Finally, rocks can be formed because of **organic**, or living, things. As an example, bituminous coal is a sedimentary rock formed from the remains of long dead plants and animals.

In this activity, you will examine several different types of sedimentary rocks, classify them according to their origin, and determine their names using a flowchart.

Fossil limestone

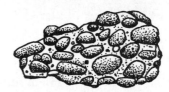

Conglomerate

Shale

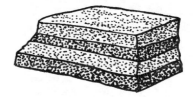

Sandstone

 MATERIALS

- Magnifying glass
- Several sedimentary rock samples (coquina, fossil limestone, breccia, conglomerate, sandstone, shale, chalk, rock gypsum, rock salt, limestone, and bituminous coal)
- Pen/pencil

(continued)

How Do Erosion, Deposition, and Cementation Form Rocks? *(continued)*

 PROCEDURE

1. You will do this activity in groups of three students. One member will record all the observations, another member will obtain rock samples from the teacher, and the third student will examine the rock specimens and lead the group in describing them.

2. When the group receives its sample, the observer will look for any visible particles in the sample. The other group members should confirm the observation. The recorder will write *yes* or *no* in the space provided on Data Table 1 in the Data Collection and Analysis section.

3. If the sample contains visible particles, use the magnifying glass and Figure 1: Sedimentary Rock Identification to try to determine what these particles are.

4. If you have determined that your sample does not contain particles, determine whether or not it is layered. Write *yes* or *no* in the space provided in Data Table 1.

5. Now, using your knowledge of sedimentary rock formation and Figure 1, determine whether the rock is **clastic** (shows rock particles) or **nonclastic** (does not show rock particles). If it is nonclastic, identify it as either **chemical** or **organic**. Then, enter this information in Data Table 1.

6. Use the flowchart in Figure 1 to identify each of the rock samples. Place the name you think belongs to the rock sample in the space provided in Data Table 1.

 DATA COLLECTION AND ANALYSIS

TABLE 1: SELECTED CHARACTERISTICS OF SEDIMENTARY ROCK SAMPLES

Rock Sample	Visible Particles? (Yes or No)	Particle Name	Layering? (Yes or No)	Organic, Chemical, or Clastic	Name of Rock
A					
B					
C					
D					
E					
F					
G					
H					
I					
J					
K					

(continued)

How Do Erosion, Deposition, and Cementation Form Rocks? *(continued)*

FIGURE 1: FLOWCHART OF SEDIMENTARY ROCK IDENTIFICATION
(Flowchart adapted from Brian Vorwald, Long Island, NY)

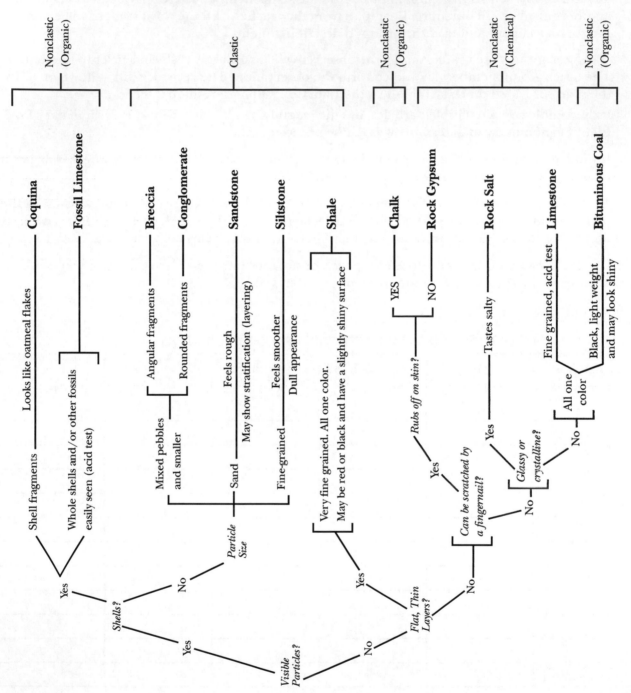

(continued)

How Do Erosion, Deposition, and Cementation Form Rocks? *(continued)*

❓ CONCLUDING QUESTIONS

1. Choose one clastic and two nonclastic rocks. Determine where each rock is most likely to have been formed. _____

   _____

   _____

   _____

   _____

2. Limestone, rock gypsum, and chalk can be hard to identify because they look alike. Describe one special property for each rock that could be used to identify it. _____

   _____

   _____

   _____

   _____

▨ Follow-up Activities ▨

1. "Brownstones" are a type of building named for the sedimentary rock used to construct them. Find out which rock these buildings are made from and write a report on "brownstones."

2. Weather erodes certain sedimentary rocks easily, while other rocks are very resistant. Create and perform an experiment to determine which common sedimentary rock is most resistant to erosion.

How Do We Test for Nutrient Minerals in Soil?

 ## INSTRUCTIONAL OBJECTIVES

Students will be able to

- examine and compare several soil types.
- identify various elemental nutrients in the soil.
- demonstrate techniques to test for and identify the presence of soil minerals.

NATIONAL SCIENCE STANDARDS ADDRESSED

Students demonstrate an understanding of

- properties of earth materials, such as minerals.
- structure and properties of matter, such as elements and compounds.
- geochemical cycles, such as conversion and movement of matter and chemical resources.
- populations and ecosystems, such as the role of decomposers in a soil environment.
- natural resource management.

Students demonstrate scientific inquiry and problem-solving skills by

- working individually and in teams to collect and share information and ideas.
- using evidence from reliable sources to develop explanations.

Students demonstrate effective scientific communication by

- representing data and results in the form of tables.

 ## MATERIALS

- Potting soil and sandy soil
- Sand, silt, and clay samples
- Hand lens
- Soil testing kit (testing for the presence of nitrogen, phosphorus, and potassium)
- Five large screwcap test tubes
- 15 medium test tubes (15 mm × 125 mm)
- 50-ml graduated cylinder
- Eyedroppers
- Test-tube rack
- Distilled water
- Plastic teaspoons
- Disposable vinyl gloves
- Stopwatch (optional)

HELPFUL HINTS AND DISCUSSION

Time frame: Two or three class periods
Structure: Cooperative learning groups of four students
Location: In a science laboratory

Use sterilized soil samples and sand, silt, and clay particles that can be purchased through major science supply companies and garden centers. Many of these science supply houses sell prepackaged soil testing kits. Each kit is designed to be used by one class. Pretesting all samples will allow you to prepare a model answer key for the macronutrient concentrations found in each soil and particle sample. If the lesson is conducted in cooperative-group format, assign each group member a specific soil or particle sample to assay for the nutrients. Demonstrate the procedures found in the instructional book for the class. Based upon your pretrial of the activity, you may need to make adjustments in particular procedures, quantities, volumes, etc. Only clean glassware and distilled water should be used in this exercise. Safety procedures must be followed.

ADAPTATIONS FOR HIGH AND LOW ACHIEVERS

High Achievers: These students should be encouraged to complete the Follow-up Activity. They should also help low achievers perform many of the required tasks.

Low Achievers: These students should be in a cooperative group with high achievers and be given a more active role in performing many of the tasks. They should also be asked to help the teacher demonstrate tasks performed in the activity.

SCORING RUBRIC

Full credit should be given to students who successfully conduct the activity in a safe manner, demonstrate proficiency in recording observations, and provide accurate, complete responses to the questions. Extra credit should be awarded to students who complete the Follow-up Activity.

 **INTERNET TIE-INS**   http://www.cals.cornell.edu/dept/flori/growon/field.html
http://markw.com/phsoil.htm

 QUIZ   1. What factors determine the differences in soil types?
2. How does the soil in a rain forest compare to the soil in a desert?
3. Describe the environmental factors that provide for nutrient-rich soil.

How Do We Test for Nutrient Minerals in Soil?

BEFORE YOU BEGIN

At one time or another, you may have potted a houseplant, tended a vegetable garden, or raised flowers. The soil these plants grew in was filled with nutrients. Just as you need nutrients for energy and proper growth, plants require the presence of nutrients in the soil. They grow best in nutrient-rich soils. Areas with warm, moist climates and lots of organisms inhabiting the earth have the richest, most fertile soils. These soils developed when physical or chemical weathering broke down rock.

Soils are classified as **topsoil**, the first 8 to 10 inches in many locations, and **subsoil**, located directly underneath the topsoil. Soil types are usually determined by the proportion of sand, silt, and clay found in them. Home gardeners, farmers, and environmentalists are interested in the nutritional value of the topsoil. This is because most crops, flowers, trees, and organism populations depend upon it for growth. As a result of weathering, soil contains many minerals classified as **macronutrients**: nitrogen (N), phosphorus (P), and potassium (K). It also contains such **micronutrients** as calcium, sulfur, magnesium, iron, boron, manganese, copper, and zinc. Soil composition varies depending on the availability and amount of each of these minerals.

Plants that grow in rain forests have different nutritional needs than plants that grow in deserts or near the ocean. This is because the soils in these different regions vary. This permits the growth of only particular plant species. In this activity, you will observe and test a variety of soils and particles for macronutrients.

 MATERIALS

- Potting soil and sandy soil
- Sand, silt, and clay samples
- Hand lens
- Soil testing kit (testing for the presence of nitrogen, phosphorus, and potassium)
- Five large screwcap test tubes
- 15 medium test tubes (15 mm × 125 mm)

- 50-ml graduated cylinder
- Eyedroppers
- Test-tube rack
- Distilled water
- Plastic teaspoons
- Disposable vinyl gloves
- Stopwatch (optional)

PROCEDURE: EXAMINING SOIL AND PARTICLE SAMPLES

1. Obtain sand, silt, and clay samples—the components of soil—from your teacher. Observe the appearance and texture of each of your samples. Use your hand lens to help you describe any specific features of each. Record these observations in the appropriate spaces in Data Table 1 of the Data Collection and Analysis section.

2. Repeat the procedure outlined above for each of your soil samples: potting soil and sandy soil. Record these observations in the appropriate spaces in Data Table 1.

(continued)

How Do We Test for Nutrient Minerals in Soil? *(continued)*

 ## PROCEDURE: PREPARING A SOIL NUTRIENT EXTRACT

1. You will prepare soil extracts for both potting soil and sandy soil to analyze for the presence of nitrogen (N), potassium (K), and phosphorus (P). **This must be performed for each of your soil and particle samples.** The amount of water, the number of testing tablets, and the time required to achieve the results for each test may vary slightly. **Remember to label all your test tubes.**

2. Test each sample for the presence and proportion of nitrogen, phosphorus, and potassium. You are using a purchased *Soil or Gardener's Testing Kit*, so it is very important to follow the directions in the instruction manual. Your teacher will review the procedures with you. The following steps represent the general directions that will guide you for this section of the activity.

3. Fill the appropriate prelabeled clean screwcap test tube with 30-ml of distilled water. Add the required number of extraction tablets (adjusted for this volume) to the tube. Screw on the cap and shake the solution until the tablets are completely dissolved.

4. Remove the cap and add one heaping teaspoon of the potting soil sample. Recap the test tube, shake well for **60 seconds**, and let the test tube stand undisturbed until the soil sample settles to the bottom of the tube (approximately 5 to 10 minutes).

5. Repeat the procedures outlined in steps 3 and 4 for the sandy soil sample and the particle samples you are testing. Make certain that you use a different prelabeled test tube for each sample.

6. Each test tube contains the **extract** (liquid) for one of your soil samples that will be used for the nitrogen, phosphorus, and potassium tests.

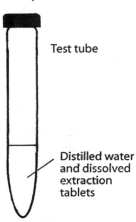

Test tube

Distilled water and dissolved extraction tablets

Procedure 3a

 ## PROCEDURE: TESTING FOR NITROGEN

1. Using a clean eyedropper, carefully take out approximately 10 ml of the extract (liquid above the soil) and transfer it to a prelabeled clean test tube.

2. Add the indicator tablet(s) provided, according to the specified directions. Then, mix well until the tablet(s) completely dissolve.

3. Wait approximately five minutes for a color to develop.

4. Compare the color (**pinkish**) of the solution to the nitrogen color chart furnished by the manufacturer on the box or on an insert card.

5. Record your results in the appropriate space in Data Table 2 of the Data Collection and Analysis section.

6. Repeat the procedures outlined in steps 1 through 5 for the remaining samples.

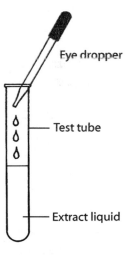

Eye dropper

Test tube

Extract liquid

Procedure 1

(continued)

How Do We Test for Nutrient Minerals in Soil? *(continued)*

 PROCEDURE: TESTING FOR PHOSPHORUS

1. Using a clean eyedropper, carefully take out approximately 2 ml (about 25 drops) of the extract and transfer it to a prelabeled clean test tube. Using a clean eyedropper, add 8 ml of distilled water to the test tube, so the total volume is approximately 10 ml.

2. Add the indicator tablet provided, according to the specified directions. Then, mix well until the tablet completely dissolves.

3. Wait approximately five minutes for a color to develop.

4. Compare the color (**bluish**) of the solution to the phosphorus color chart furnished by the manufacturer on the box or on an insert card.

5. Record your results in the appropriate space in Data Table 2.

6. Repeat the procedures outlined in steps 1 through 5 for the remaining samples.

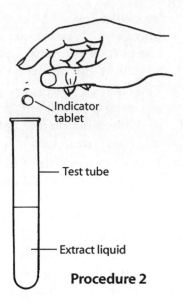

Indicator tablet

Test tube

Extract liquid

Procedure 2

 PROCEDURE: TESTING FOR POTASSIUM

1. Using a clean eyedropper, carefully take out approximately 10 ml of the extract and transfer it to a prelabeled clean test tube.

2. Add the indicator tablet provided, according to the specified directions. Then, mix well until the tablet completely dissolves.

3. Wait approximately one minute for a color to develop.

4. Compare the **cloudiness** of the solution to the potassium color chart furnished by the manufacturer on the box or on an insert card.

5. Record your results in the appropriate space in Data Table 2.

6. Repeat the procedures outlined in steps 1 through 5 for the remaining samples.

 DATA COLLECTION AND ANALYSIS

DATA TABLE 1: STUDENT DESCRIPTIONS OF CHARACTERISTICS OF SAND, SILT, CLAY, AND SOIL SAMPLES

Sample	Appearance Characteristics	Feel and Texture
Sand		
Silt		
Clay		
Potting Soil		
Sandy Soil		

(continued)

How Do We Test for Nutrient Minerals in Soil? *(continued)*

DATA TABLE 2: RESULTS OF STUDENT TESTS
FOR THE PRESENCE OF MACRONUTRIENT MINERALS IN SOIL SAMPLES

Sample	Nitrogen	Phosphorus	Potassium
Potting Soil			
Sandy Soil			
Sand			
Silt			
Clay			

CONCLUDING QUESTIONS

1. Compare the particle materials that you examined in this exercise. _____

_____

_____

_____

2. How did the appearance and texture of the potting soil differ from that of the sandy soil?

_____

_____

3. Which soil sample contained the highest percentage of each nutrient? Which samples would you classify as nutrient rich? Explain your answer._____

_____

_____

▨ Follow-up Activity ▨

Do the same exercise using a clayey soil, loamy soil, and soil from your garden or local area. These soil types typically vary in their proportions of sand, silt, and clay. Use the same procedures described in the activity to test for the concentration of macronutrients: nitrogen, phosphorus, and potassium.

How Do Seeds Grow in Different Environments?

 INSTRUCTIONAL OBJECTIVES

Students will be able to

- examine and compare several soil types.
- practice seed germination skills.
- compare and describe seed growth in various soil environments.

 NATIONAL SCIENCE STANDARDS ADDRESSED

Students demonstrate an understanding of

- geochemical cycles, such as chemical resources.
- interdependence of organisms, such as the conservation of matter.
- natural resource management.

Students demonstrate scientific inquiry and problem-solving skills by

- working individually and in teams to collect and share information and ideas.
- using variables in an experiment.

Students demonstrate effective scientific communication by

- representing data and results in the form of tables and graphs.

 MATERIALS

- Potting soil, sandy soil, and sand
- Hand lens
- Distilled water
- Lima bean seeds
- Planting pots (peat, plastic, or clay), 3 to 4 inches tall

HELPFUL HINTS AND DISCUSSION

Time frame: Two class periods preparing for seed germination and 10 days for subsequent plant growth

Structure: Cooperative learning groups of four students

Location: In a science laboratory

Use sterilized soil samples that can be purchased through major science supply companies and garden centers. Only distilled water is to be used in this exercise. Make sure that students understand that different soil types have different water retention abilities.

ADAPTATIONS FOR HIGH AND LOW ACHIEVERS

High Achievers: These students should be encouraged to complete the Follow-up Activity. These students should also help low achievers to perform many of the required tasks.

Low Achievers: These students should be in a cooperative group with high achievers and be given a more active role in performing many of the tasks.

SCORING RUBRIC

Full credit should be given to students who successfully conduct the activity in a safe manner, demonstrate proficiency in recording observations, and provide accurate complete responses to the questions. Extra credit should be awarded to students who complete the Follow-up Activity.

 INTERNET TIE-INS   http://www.petrik.com/PUBLIC/library/ups.html
http://www.swcs.org/t_resources_critical_Fact.htm

 QUIZ   1. What factors determine the differences among soil types?
2. How does the size of air spaces between soil particles affect the soil's ability to retain water?
3. In which soil sample (potting soil or sandy soil) do lima beans grow best? Explain your answer.

Name _____   Date _____

How Do Seeds Grow in Different Environments?

 BEFORE YOU BEGIN

A variety of physical and chemical processes were at work for long periods of time to grind rocks into soil. Soils are composed of these weathered rock particles and organic matter. Soil composition varies. Some soils are very sandy, some are made of clay, and soils found in the tropics contain mostly organic materials. Soils are classified by their mineral content, the type and amount of organic matter, and their ability to hold water. The kinds of plants found in an area depend in part on the type of soil found in the area. In this activity, you will observe the germination of seeds and the growth of seedlings in potting soil and sandy soil. Potting soil has a high proportion of clay, some organic matter, and, of course, sand. As a general rule, sandy soils do **not** hold water as well as potting soils.

 MATERIALS

- Potting soil, sandy soil, and sand
- Hand lens
- Distilled water

- Lima bean seeds
- Planting pots (peat, plastic, or clay), 3 to 4 inches tall

 PROCEDURE

1. Obtain sand, potting soil, and sandy soil samples from your teacher. Observe the appearance and texture of each sample at your station. Use your hand lens to help you describe specific features of each one. Record these observations in the appropriate spaces in Data Table 1 of the Data Collection and Analysis section.

2. After examining the soil samples, fill six pots for planting: two pots of potting soil, two pots of sandy soil, and two pots of sand.

3. Place four lima bean seeds into each pot. Cover the seeds with approximately one-quarter inch of the appropriate soil type. Water each of your pots with distilled water only. **Tap water usually contains dissolved minerals and salts.**

4. Place your potted seeds in a warm, sunny location. Water each of your pots every day.

5. For 10 days, examine each of your experimental pots daily for seed germination and subsequent seedling growth.

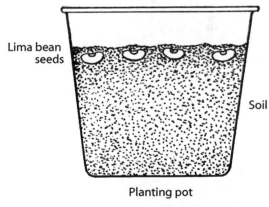

Lima bean seeds

Soil

Planting pot

Procedure 3

(continued)

How Do Seeds Grow in Different Environments? *(continued)*

6. Record all observations each day for all 10 days in Data Table 2 of the Data Collection and Analysis section. Take careful note of the germination time, the number of seedlings that germinate, the average height of the seedlings in each pot, the length of the leaves, and any other observations you care to make.

7. Make sketches of your seedlings at the end of the 10-day period in Data Table 2. You should clearly illustrate the differences in appearance of the plants in the different soil.

8. Graph the height of the seedlings in each soil type for each of the 10 days, using the line graph in Figure 1 of the Data Collection and Analysis section.

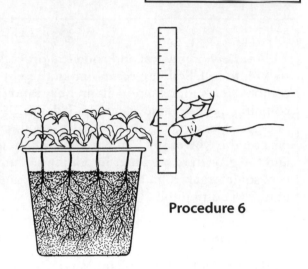

Procedure 6

9. You will need to determine a scale for the *y*-axis, based on your shortest and tallest seedling measurements. Each planting soil medium will have its own set of points for each day's average height measurement (0 days through 10 days).

10. Use three different colored pencils, one to draw the graph for each planting soil. Enter the points for each soil type and then draw a line to connect the points.

DATA COLLECTION AND ANALYSIS

DATA TABLE 1: STUDENT DESCRIPTIONS OF CHARACTERISTICS OF POTTING SOIL, SANDY SOIL, AND SAND

Sample	Appearance	Feel and Texture
Potting Soil		
Sandy Soil		
Sand		

(continued)

Name _____ Date _____

DATA TABLE 2: STUDENT DESCRIPTIONS OF SEEDLING GROWTH OF LIMA BEANS IN DIFFERENT SOILS

Sample	Your Observations		Your Illustrations
Potting Soil	Day 1		
	Day 2		
	Day 3		
	Day 4		
	Day 5		
	Day 6		
	Day 7		
	Day 8		
	Day 9		
	Day 10		
Sandy Soil	Day 1		
	Day 2		
	Day 3		
	Day 4		
	Day 5		
	Day 6		
	Day 7		
	Day 8		
	Day 9		
	Day 10		
Sand	Day 1		
	Day 2		
	Day 3		
	Day 4		
	Day 5		
	Day 6		
	Day 7		
	Day 8		
	Day 9		
	Day 10		

(continued)

How Do Seeds Grow in Different Environments? *(continued)*

FIGURE 1: GROWTH OF SEEDLINGS IN DIFFERENT ENVIRONMENTS

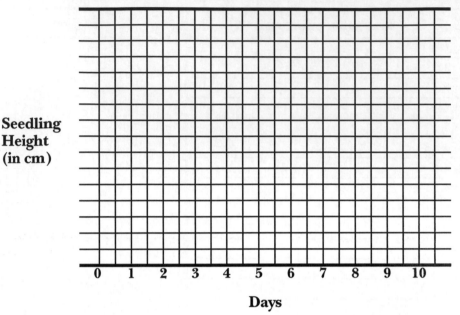

Seedling
Height
(in cm)

0 1 2 3 4 5 6 7 8 9 10

Days

? CONCLUDING QUESTIONS

1. Why is it important to germinate your seeds with distilled water rather than tap water? _____
   _____
   _____

2. Based on the growth of your seedlings, which soil sample provided the best medium for plant
   growth? How do you account for these results? _____
   _____
   _____

3. Compare the size and number of leaves on the seedlings in each soil type._____
   _____
   _____
   _____

 **Follow-up Activity**

Do the same exercise using a clayey soil, loamy soil, and soil from your garden or local area. These
soil types typically vary in their proportions of sand, silt, and clay. Germinate and grow lima bean
(or other) seeds to see whether these plants flourish in these different types of soils.

How Can We Determine the Age of Rocks?

 ## INSTRUCTIONAL OBJECTIVES

Students will be able to

- record and analyze data.
- compare the mathematics of probability to radioactive half-life.
- relate half-life to radioactive dating.
- construct a model to visualize the process of radioactive decay.

 ## NATIONAL SCIENCE STANDARDS ADDRESSED

Students demonstrate an understanding of

- Earth's history, such as change over time and fossil evidence.
- structure of atoms, such as radioactivity.
- energy in earth systems, such as radioactive decay.

Students demonstrate scientific inquiry and problem-solving skills by

- working in teams to collect and share information.
- identifying the outcomes of an investigation.

Students demonstrate competence with the tools and techniques of science by

- collecting and analyzing data using concepts and such techniques as probability and reliability.

 ## MATERIALS

- Shoe box with cover
- 80 pennies
- Pen/pencil

HELPFUL HINTS AND DISCUSSION

Time frame: One or two class periods
Structure: Cooperative learning groups of two students
Location: In a classroom or laboratory

Before beginning this activity, be sure to define such terms as radioactivity, half-life, and isotope. Explain to students the importance of placing all pennies heads up at the beginning of the experiment and of leaving the pennies outside of the shoe box once they have been removed. For another twist on this activity, teachers can substitute M & M's for the pennies.

ADAPTATIONS FOR HIGH AND LOW ACHIEVERS

High Achievers: These students should be encouraged to carry out all Follow-up Activities. They should also work with low achievers.

Low Achievers: These students should work with the high achievers and/or adults. Use of the M & M's would also be recommended.

SCORING RUBRIC

Full credit should be given to those students who accurately record observations and provide correct answers in full sentences to the questions. Extra credit may be given if any of the Follow-up Activities are completed satisfactorily.

 ## INTERNET TIE-INS

http://cdl-flylab.sonoma.edu/edesktop/VirtApps/VirtualEarthQuake/VQuakeIntro.html
http://helios.augustana.edu/~kdv/rdecay.html
http://www.exploratorium.edu/xref/exhibits/radioactive_decay_model.html

 ## QUIZ

1. How can some radioactive elements be used to identify the age of a rock?
2. What is a half-life?

Name _____   Date _____

How Can We Determine the Age of Rocks?

 BEFORE YOU BEGIN

How can we know the age of the Earth if no human was alive at the beginning? The history of the Earth is told in some rocks that we can find today. Some of these rocks contain **radioisotopes**. Radioisotopes are elements that contain atoms in an unstable state. In order to become stable, the atoms of these elements change into the atoms of other elements. This process is known as **radioactive decay**.

Scientists have been able to determine how long it takes for half of the atoms in a given amount of each radioactive element to decay into the atoms of a more stable element. This amount of radioactive decay is known as a **half-life**.

Carbon 14 is one example of a radioactive element. It is an unstable **isotope** of the element carbon. As long as a plant or animal is alive, the amount of carbon 14 in its body is kept in balance. If the organism needs more carbon 14, it is replaced from the air and soil. However, when an organism dies, carbon 14 is no longer replenished, and it begins to decay. Scientists have determined that half of a given amount of carbon 14 atoms take 5700 years to change into nitrogen 14, which is stable. Therefore, the half-life of carbon 14 is 5700 years.

In this activity, you will use pennies to represent the radioactive decay of an imaginary element, headsium. You will then collect data and prepare graphs to visualize the process of radioactive decay.

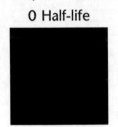

0 Half-life	1 Half-life	2 Half-lives	3 Half-lives	4 Half-lives
Carbon 14 Radiosotope No Decay Product	$\frac{1}{2}$ Carbon 14 Radiosotope $\frac{1}{2}$ Decay Product (Nitrogen 14)	$\frac{1}{4}$ Carbon 14 Radiosotope $\frac{3}{4}$ Decay Product (Nitrogen 14)	$\frac{1}{8}$ Carbon 14 Radiosotope $\frac{7}{8}$ Decay Product (Nitrogen 14)	$\frac{1}{16}$ Carbon 14 Radiosotope $\frac{15}{16}$ Decay Product (Nitrogen 14)

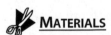 MATERIALS

- Shoe box with cover
- 80 pennies

- Pen/pencil

(continued)

How Can We Determine the Age of Rocks? *(continued)*

 PROCEDURES

1. In your group of two, one of you will be responsible for shaking the box of pennies, and the other will count and remove the pennies representing decayed atoms.

2. You will receive 80 pennies and a shoe box with a cover from your teacher. Place the 80 pennies heads up in the shoe box. The heads of these pennies represent the atoms of the radioisotope element "headsium."

3. Place the cover on the shoe box and have the shaker shake the box vigorously four times, using an up and down motion.

4. Remove the pennies that are tails up from the box. They represent the atoms of radioactive "headsium" that have decayed into stable "tailsium." Record the number of "headsium" and "tailsium" atoms in the table in the Data Collection and Analysis section. Replace the cover on the shoe box.

5. Repeat steps 3 and 4 three more times. Each time, remove the "tailsium" pennies from the shoe box, and record the number of "headsium" and "tailsium" pennies in the Data Collection and Analysis section.

6. Prepare a line graph of the number of "headsium" and "tailsium" atoms (their half lives). Use a solid line to represent "headsium" and a dashed line to represent "tailsium."

7. After your class has completed the activity, your teacher will draw the table entitled "Decay of Headsium (Class)" on the board. Then, one member of each group will enter its data on the table.

8. Finally, enter the information on the graph grid entitled "Class Average of the Decay of Headsium," which your teacher has placed on the board.

 DATA COLLECTION AND ANALYSIS

DECAY OF HEADSIUM (INDIVIDUAL)

Number of Trials	Number of Headsium Atoms	Number of Tailsium Atoms	Half Lives
0	80	0	0
1			
2			
3			
4			

(continued)

How Can We Determine the Age of Rocks? *(continued)*

DECAY OF HEADSIUM (INDIVIDUAL): NUMBER OF HEADSIUM AND TAILSIUM ATOMS AFTER EACH TRIAL (HALF LIVES)

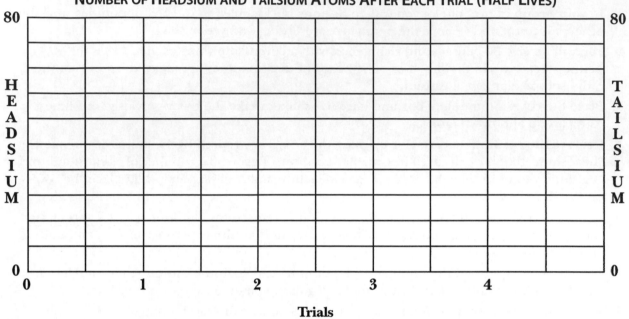

Trials

DECAY OF HEADSIUM (CLASS): NUMBER OF HEADSIUM LEFT

Trial Number	Group Number							Total	Class Average
	1	2	3	4	5	6	7		
0									
1									
2									
3									
4									

(continued)

How Can We Determine the Age of Rocks? *(continued)*

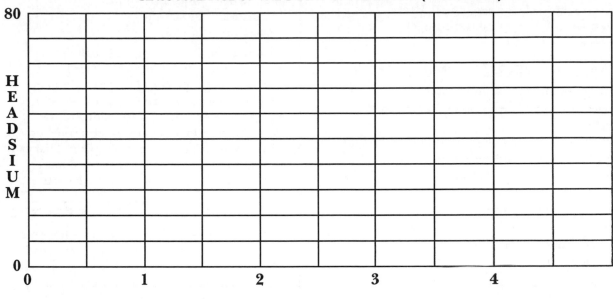

CLASS AVERAGE OF THE DECAY OF HEADSIUM (HALF LIVES)

Trials (Half Lives)

❓ CONCLUDING QUESTIONS

1. Describe two ways in which this activity models what takes place during radioactive decay.

   _____

   _____

2. Why was the class data more like radioactive decay than your individual data? _____

   _____

   _____

3. A student changes this experiment by using 2,400 dimes. If 75 heads remain in the box, how many trials do you think have been done? Explain your answer. _____

   _____

   _____

▦ Follow-up Activities ▦

1. Research the tools that scientists use to determine the age of fossils. Write a report and present it to your class.
2. Create an experiment to determine if the number of pennies used affects the outcome of this activity.

How Do We Use Rocks to Examine Geologic History?

 INSTRUCTIONAL OBJECTIVES

Students will be able to

- describe the relative age of rock layers.
- identify rock layers of differing ages and compositions.

 NATIONAL SCIENCE STANDARDS ADDRESSED

Students demonstrate an understanding of

- structure of the earth system, such as rock cycles.
- Earth's history, such as earth processes including change over time and fossil evidence.
- big ideas and unifying concepts, such as change and consistency, cause and effect.

Students demonstrate scientific inquiry and problem-solving skills by

- using evidence from reliable sources to develop models.

Students demonstrate effective scientific communication by

- representing data in multiple ways including diagrams.

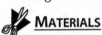 **MATERIALS**

- Pen or pencil

HELPFUL HINTS AND DISCUSSION

Time frame: One class period
Structure: Individuals
Location: In class

In this activity, students will analyze data collected during the drilling of oil wells and create a geologic profile of the area. Students should have already been taught the ideas of geologic time and the relative dating of rock layers. Teachers may want to create a collaborative activity using this activity as a template. That can be done by grouping the students and having them create a geologic profile for a large area.

ADAPTATIONS FOR HIGH AND LOW ACHIEVERS

High Achievers: Encourage these students to use the Internet or other sources of information to examine the geologic profile of the local area. Students should then create and present a report to class based on their work.

Low Achievers: These students may need an adult's or teacher's help in plotting the location of different rock layers on the map.

SCORING RUBRIC

Full credit should be given to students who create a correct geologic profile for the three oil wells and answer all analysis questions successfully.

  INTERNET TIE-INS   http://woodshole.er.usgs.gov/epubs/bolide/

QUIZ
1. What methods can be used to determine the different ages of rock layers?
2. How can the age of a rock layer be identified by comparing it to the rock layers above and below it?
3. Describe how fossils can be used to compare rock layers located several hundred miles apart.

How Do We Use Rocks to Examine Geologic History?

BEFORE YOU BEGIN

Based on geologic evidence, scientists estimate that the Earth is approximately 4.5 billion years old. One piece of supporting evidence is the thickness of the rock layers. Most geologists believe that it would have taken that much time to create all of the layers of rock found on Earth. To estimate the age of the Earth, scientists perform experiments to determine how long it takes to create a meter of layered rock. They then multiply this time by the actual thickness of the Earth's rock layers.

Within these rock layers is a record of events that have occurred on Earth. They also contain the remains and/or imprints of the different plants and animals that have lived on Earth. By understanding some simple rules about rock-layer formation, we can use the layers to measure the time that has passed since the creation of the Earth. One important fact to remember is that rock layers form horizontally. Even if they are deposited on a slope, the rock layers will form in horizontal bands. A second important factor is that the older rock layers will be found farther beneath the surface, while younger layers will be closer to the top. This allows us to date rock layers based on their comparative positions underground. This is known as **relative age**. Finally, we can use fossils or radioactive minerals found in a rock layer to determine the **absolute age** of the layer.

In this activity, you will use data collected during the process of drilling for oil to construct a side view of the rock layers found underground at the drilling location. This side view is known as a **geologic profile**.

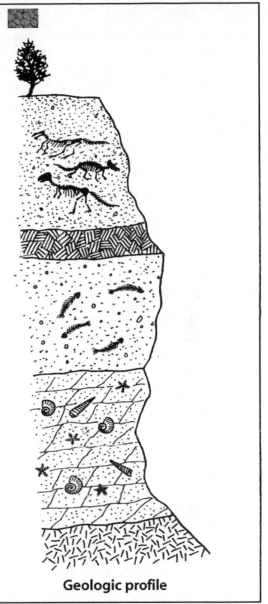

Geologic profile

 **MATERIALS**

- Pen or pencil

(continued)

Name _____   Date _____

PROCEDURES

1. While drilling for oil at three sites, a geologist collected samples of the rocks found at different layers underground. Whenever the drill hit a new type of rock, the geologist collected a sample and determined the depth at which it was found. Some of the rock samples contained fossils and/or radioactive minerals. The geologist then created a record of her findings, shown on Table 1.

2. At each drilling site marked on Table 2, place a small horizontal line at the depths where Table 1 tells you that each type of rock layer was found. After making the horizontal line, write the name of the type of rock on the line. The first piece of data has already been plotted and labeled for you as a sample: the sandstone found at a depth of 100 feet at Oil Well A.

3. After you have plotted all of the data, use a ruler to connect the areas on all three wells where the rock types are the same. Your lines should be continuous across the entire page. When you reach a point where there is no data, draw a dotted line to indicate the continuing rock layers.

4. Write in the name of the rock found at these depths directly above the dotted line that you just created.

5. Use the notes provided by the geologist for all three oil wells to determine the age of the rock layers. Then, complete the information in Data Table 3. The notes contain all the information you need to determine the age of each rock layer. The first one has been done for you as a sample.

6. Put your rock layers in order from youngest (1) to oldest (11) and place these numbers in Table 2 to the left of Oil Well A. Number 1 has been done as a sample for you to follow.

(continued)

Name _____ Date _____

DATA COLLECTION AND ANALYSIS

TABLE 1: DEPTH, TYPE OF ROCK, AND GEOLOGIST'S NOTES FOR OIL WELLS A, B, AND C

Oil Well A

Depth (Ft)	Rock	Notes
100	Sandstone	Radioactive dating—1.6 million years old
189	Shale	
206	Conglomerate	Fossil remains—67 million years old
250	Sandstone	
340	Shale	
466	Breccia	Fossil remains— 245 million years old
550	Sandstone	
625	Marble	
700	Schist	
790	Basalt	Radioactive dating— 420 million years old
875	Basalt	Radioactive dating— 475 million years old

Oil Well B

Depth (Ft)	Rock	Notes
100	Shale	Fossil remains—36 million years old
160	Conglomerate	
225	Sandstone	
260	Shale	
450	Breccia	
510	Sandstone	Radioactive dating— 295 million years old
600	Marble	Fossil remains— 325 million years old
700	Schist	Radioactive dating— 400 million years old
760	Basalt	
850	Basalt	

Oil Well C

Depth (Ft)	Rock	Notes
100	Shale	
160	Conglomerate	
250	Sandstone	Fossil remains— 150 million years old
300	Shale	??? Cannot be determined
450	Breccia	
525	Sandstone	
575	Marble	

(continued)

How Do We Use Rocks to Examine Geologic History? *(continued)*

TABLE 2

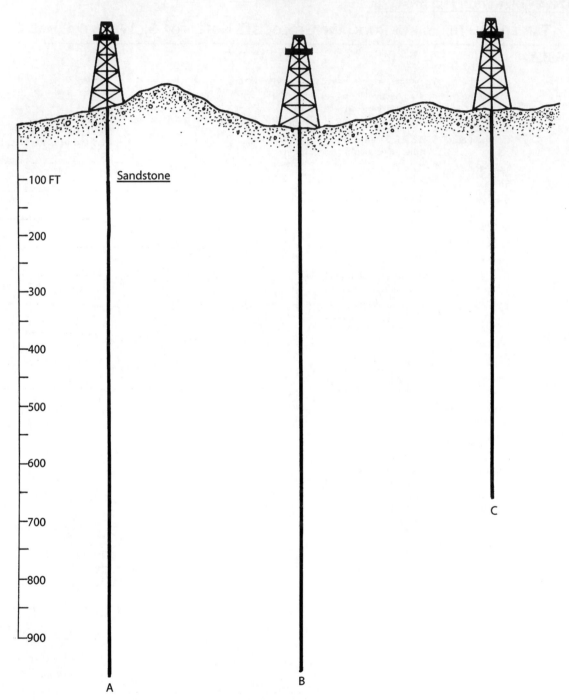

Sandstone

100 FT

200

300

400

500

600

700

800

900

A   B   C

Figure 1

(continued)

How Do We Use Rocks to Examine Geologic History? *(continued)*

TABLE 3: DETERMINATION OF THE GEOLOGIC AGE OF ROCK LAYERS

Number of Rock Layer	Era	Period	Age Determined by Geologist	Method Used to Determine Age	Name of Rock Layer
1	Cenozoic	Quaternary	1.6 million years	Radioactive dating	Sandstone
2					
3					
4					
5					
6					
7					
8					
9					
10					
11					

TABLE 4: GEOLOGIC TIME TABLE

Millions of Years Ago	Era	Period
0–1.8	Cenozoic	Quaternary
1.8–65	Cenozoic	Tertiary
65–141	Mesozoic	Cretaceous
141–195	Mesozoic	Jurassic
195–230	Mesozoic	Triassic
230–280	Paleozoic	Permian
280–310	Paleozoic	Pennsylvanian
310–345	Paleozoic	Mississippian
345–395	Paleozoic	Devonian
395–435	Paleozoic	Silurian
435–500	Paleozoic	Ordovician
500–570	Paleozoic	Cambrian

(continued)

How Do We Use Rocks to Examine Geologic History? *(continued)*

? CONCLUDING QUESTIONS

1. Which rock layer cannot have its absolute age determined in this activity? Is there any other way to find out the age of this layer? Explain your answer. _____

   _____

   _____

   _____

   _____

2. Were all similar rock layers found at the same depth? How can you explain any similar rock layers that were not found at exactly the same depth? _____

   _____

   _____

   _____

   _____

3. What is the difference between the relative age of a rock layer and its absolute age? _____

   _____

   _____

   _____

   _____

Follow-up Activities

1. Find geologic maps of your local area and create a geologic profile. Present this profile to the class.
2. Contact a local oil or gas drilling company to discuss their methods of collecting data on the rock layers underground. Write a report and present this to the class.

How Are Fossil Imprints of Plant Leaves Formed?

 INSTRUCTIONAL OBJECTIVES

Students will be able to

- prepare impressions of several plant leaves.
- observe and compare evolutionary characteristics of the leaf structures of flowering and nonflowering plants from "fossilized" imprints.
- analyze fossil evidence in the rock record.
- interpret a *Geologic Timetable* reference scale.

NATIONAL SCIENCE STANDARDS ADDRESSED

Students demonstrate an understanding of

- structure and function of living systems, such as leaf structure.
- properties of earth materials, such as sedimentary rocks and minerals.
- Earth's history, such as change over time and fossil evidence.
- origin and evolution of the earth system, such as geologic time and the age of life forms.

Students demonstrate scientific inquiry and problem-solving skills by

- working individually and in teams to collect and share information and ideas.
- classifying the outcome of an investigation by interpreting a fossil record.

Students demonstrate effective scientific communication by

- representing data and results in the form of tables, drawings, diagrams, and artwork.

 MATERIALS

- Several identifiable leaves (for example, oak, maple, geranium, fern, pine needles) from nonflowering and flowering plant species
- Plaster of paris or a suitable imprint-creating substance
- Water
- Disposable 9-inch aluminum pan
- Large mixing bowl or small paint bucket, wooden paint stick
- Spatula
- Centimeter ruler

- Laboratory apron, disposable vinyl or latex gloves, safety goggles
- *Geologic Timetable* reference scale

HELPFUL HINTS AND DISCUSSION

Time frame: Two class periods, depending upon how many leaf imprints are produced

Structure: Collaborative learning groups of four students

Location: In a science laboratory

Use easily identifiable leaves with a firm structure to allow for a more viable imprint to be cast in the plaster. These leaves should represent various stages of plant evolution including nonflowering plants (ferns), cone-bearing plants (pine, spruce, fir), flowering plants (geranium), and trees (maple, oak). As a prelab activity, you should demonstrate the technique of impression formation to the class, since students will need hands-on assistance while working with plaster of paris, which can set quickly. Some science supply companies sell imprint-creating materials that can be used in place of plaster of paris. Be certain to prepare a separate answer key for each group. If the lesson is conducted in cooperative-group format, assign each group member a particular task in the preparation of the imprint design.

⑤ Safety procedures must be followed, particularly when using plaster of paris, and ample clean-up time must be provided.

ADAPTATIONS FOR HIGH AND LOW ACHIEVERS

High Achievers: These students should be encouraged to complete the Follow-up Activity. They should also help low achievers perform many of the required tasks.

Low Achievers: These students should be in a cooperative group with high achievers and be given a more active role in performing many of the tasks. They should also be asked to help the teacher demonstrate tasks performed in the activity.

SCORING RUBRIC

Full credit should be given to students who successfully conduct the activity in a safe manner, demonstrate proficiency in recording observations, and provide accurate, complete responses to the questions. Extra credit should be awarded to students who complete the Follow-up Activity.

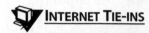

INTERNET TIE-INS   http://www.nmnh.si.edu/VirtualTour/Tour/First/FossilPlants/index.html
http://www.ucmp.berkeley.edu/plants/plantaefr.html

QUIZ   1. Identify and explain two ways in which organic matter is fossilized.
2. Explain why the original remains of plants are rarely preserved.
3. How are fossils preserved without the original remains intact?

Name _____ Date _____

How Are Fossil Imprints of Plant Leaves Formed?

 BEFORE YOU BEGIN

Scientists and students alike have always been curious about the past. For example, paleontologists try to recreate the history of life on Earth from fossils they find in rocks. Fossil remains, usually found in sedimentary rock, occur in various forms and provide evidence and clues for scientists to study. Fossils exist in the following forms:

- original remains of an organism— for example, its bones and/or teeth
- a whole organism, such as an insect, preserved in a sticky resin called amber
- petrified remains, when the original organic material has been replaced by minerals— for example, petrified wood
- molds and casts of the original plants or animals
- imprints left by the original organisms, such as footprints

It is this last type of fossil evidence, **imprints** found in sedimentary rock layers, that gives us most of our information about plants that existed long ago. In this activity, you will prepare imprints of several leaf species. You will use these to study the evolution of plants using a fossil record. Using reference materials, you will approximate the time and possible environmental conditions during which these plants first appeared and thrived on the Earth.

 MATERIALS

- Several identifiable leaves (for example, oak, maple, geranium, fern, pine needles) from nonflowering and flowering plant species
- Plaster of paris or a suitable imprint-creating substance
- Water
- Disposable 9-inch aluminum pan

- Large mixing bowl or small paint bucket, wooden paint stick
- Spatula
- Centimeter ruler
- Laboratory apron, disposable vinyl or latex gloves, safety goggles
- *Geologic Timetable* reference scale

PROCEDURES

1. Prepare a plaster of paris slurry according to the manufacturer's directions. Continue to add small amounts of water to achieve a uniform consistency, without lumps. Check with your teacher to be certain that the plaster is ready to use. **You should wear disposable gloves and a laboratory apron to protect your clothing and your skin.**

2. Carefully pour this mixture into a 9-inch disposable aluminum pan until it reaches close to the top of the pan. Let this mixture slowly settle, gently shifting the pan back and forth on your table top to achieve an even mixing. Use your spatula to smooth out the top, if necessary.

(continued)

How Are Fossil Imprints of Plant Leaves Formed? *(continued)*

3. Use a spatula to lightly score the surface of plaster down the middle, producing two equal halves. Rotate the pan 90 degrees and score again to produce four equal quarters. Each quarter section of the cast will be for the leaf imprint of a different plant species. Be certain to make a key that allows you to keep track of which leaf species has been used in which quarter.

4. Write down the name of your leaf specimens in the appropriate spaces in Data Table 1 of the Data Collection and Analysis section.

5. Gently press the top side of your first leaf specimen into the hardening plaster in the upper left quarter of the pan. Do not disturb the surrounding material. Use the flat side of the spatula to help apply light pressure to the leaf in the plaster.

6. Repeat the procedure outlined above for each of the other leaf specimens, continuing through the remaining quarters in a clockwise direction.

7. As the plaster of paris begins to harden, carefully lift up each leaf without disturbing the surrounding plaster. Discard the used leaves in an appropriate trash container.

Example of leaf imprint

8. After the plaster has completely hardened (set), carefully outline the leaf structures with a fine felt-tip marker.

9. Sketch each leaf "imprint" in the spaces provided in Figures 1, 2, 3, and 4 of the Data Collection and Analysis section.

10. To find the size of your leaf from its imprint, measure the **length** (from base of leaf to the tip) and the **width** (at the widest point) in centimeters *to the nearest tenth*. Record these measurements in the appropriate spaces in Data Table 1 of the Data Collection and Analysis section.

11. List any distinguishing characteristics of your specimen—such as leaf margin, shape, and vein pattern—in the appropriate spaces in Data Table 1. You may wish to use a book on tree identification to help distinguish the different characteristics of leaves.

12. Using a *Geologic Timetable,* identify the **era** and **period** when your plant specimen first appeared on Earth. Then, determine when it thrived as a dominant species. Record these findings in the appropriate spaces in Data Table 1.

(continued)

How Are Fossil Imprints of Plant Leaves Formed? *(continued)*

 DATA COLLECTION AND ANALYSIS

DATA TABLE 1: RESULTS OF STUDYING THE "FOSSIL" IMPRINT OF A LEAF

Leaf Specimen	Length (in cm.)	Width (in cm.)	Distinguishing Characteristics	Era (1st/dominant)	Period (1st/dominant)

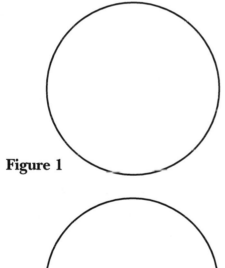

Figure 1

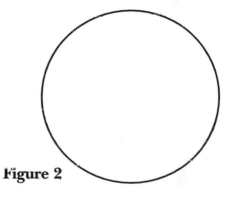

Figure 2

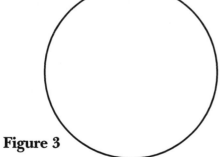

Figure 3

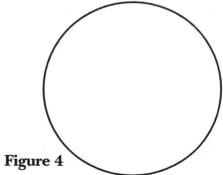

Figure 4

(continued)

How Are Fossil Imprints of Plant Leaves Formed? *(continued)*

❓ CONCLUDING QUESTIONS

1. Explain how leaves, which are soft, can leave imprints in sedimentary rocks.

   _____

   _____

   _____

   _____

2. From your results and the *Geologic Timetable,* identify the specimen that appeared most recently on Earth. Describe the leaf pattern, and compare its structure to one from an earlier time.

   _____

   _____

   _____

   _____

   _____

3. Explain how fossils provide information that allows us to trace the evolutionary history of plants on the Earth. _____

   _____

   _____

   _____

   _____

▒ Follow-up Activity ▒

Research and prepare a flowchart to illustrate the evolutionary path of plants. Include stem structures and leaf patterns. Write a description of each species studied, and include a diagram of each plant variety described. You should discuss spores, cones, and flowers, and their role in the reproduction of each plant.

INSTRUCTIONAL OBJECTIVES

Students will be able to

- produce a fossil record using "animal" tracks.
- interpret fossil evidence in the rock record.
- analyze the walking stride of a dinosaur species.
- interpret a *Geologic Timetable* reference scale.

 NATIONAL SCIENCE STANDARDS ADDRESSED

Students demonstrate an understanding of

- properties of earth materials.
- Earth's history, such as change over time and fossil evidence.
- origin and evolution of the earth system, such as geologic time and the age of life forms.

Students demonstrate scientific inquiry and problem-solving skills by

- working individually and in teams to collect and share information and ideas.
- classifying the outcome of an investigation by interpreting a fossil record.

Students demonstrate effective scientific communication by

- representing data and results in the form of tables, drawings, diagrams, and artwork.

 MATERIALS

- Several species of two-footed rubber or plastic dinosaur models 5 to 7 inches tall
- Plaster of paris or a suitable imprint-creating substance
- Water
- Disposable 9-inch aluminum pan
- Aluminum foil
- Large mixing bowl or small paint bucket, wooden paint stick
- Spatula
- Centimeter ruler
- Laboratory apron, disposable vinyl or latex gloves, safety goggles
- *Geologic Timetable* reference scale

HELPFUL HINTS AND DISCUSSION

Time frame: Two class periods, depending upon how many fossil dinosaur tracks are produced

Structure: Cooperative learning groups of four students

Location: In a science laboratory

Use realistic looking, medium-sized plastic or rubber dinosaur models to allow for a more viable footprint to be cast in the plaster. Various two-footed (bipedal) specimens should be included to represent a variety of eras and periods in the evolution of several dinosaur and/or reptile species. As a prelab activity, you should demonstrate the technique of impression formation to the class, since students will need hands-on assistance while working with plaster of paris, which can set quickly. Some science supply companies sell imprint-creating materials that can be used in place of plaster of paris. Be certain to prepare a separate answer key for each group. If the lesson is conducted in cooperative-group format, assign each group member a particular task in the preparation of the footprint impression design.
 Safety procedures must be followed, particularly when using plaster of paris, and ample clean-up time must be provided.

ADAPTATIONS FOR HIGH AND LOW ACHIEVERS

High Achievers: These students should be encouraged to complete the Follow-up Activity. They should also help low achievers perform many of the required tasks.

Low Achievers: These students should be in a cooperative group with high achievers and be given a more active role in performing many of the tasks. They should also be asked to help the teacher demonstrate tasks performed in the activity.

SCORING RUBRIC

Full credit should be given to students who successfully conduct the activity, demonstrate proficiency in recording observations, and provide accurate, complete responses to the questions. Extra credit should be awarded to students who complete the Follow-up Activity.

  **INTERNET TIE-INS**   http://www.ucmp.berkeley.edu/diapsids/dinosaur.html
http://www.emory.edu/COLLEGE/ENVS/research/ichnology/dinotraces.html

QUIZ   1. Why are dinosaur footprints found only in sedimentary rock?
2. How would scientists use the walking stride of dinosaurs to help calculate their size?
3. A paleontologist discovers footprints from several dinosaur species in a sedimentary rock layer. Explain how these animal tracks might provide clues to the live dinosaurs.

Name _____   Date _____

▓▓ BEFORE YOU BEGIN ▓▓

People have always been fascinated by dinosaurs. Scientists called paleontologists study dinosaur bones and footprints in the fossil record to find out about dinosaurs. They also learn about the geologic history of the Earth as they study the sedimentary rock that contains the fossils. Sedimentary, or layered, rock is where many fossil remains of dinosaurs are found. The fossils include bones, teeth, and fossilized eggs. These forms of evidence allow scientists to analyze the life history of these creatures. Jaw patterns and teeth may reveal the feeding habits of dinosaurs. Such structures as armored plates and spiked tails provide clues to how dinosaurs defended themselves. Dinosaur footprints and tracks give scientists more information about the way dinosaurs lived. In this activity, you will prepare a **dino-track**, a series of footprints of a dinosaur, to model what we might find in the fossil record. Then, using reference materials, you will determine when these animals lived.

MATERIALS

- Several species of two-footed rubber or plastic dinosaur models 5 to 7 inches tall
- Plaster of paris or a suitable imprint-creating substance
- Water
- Disposable 9-inch aluminum pan
- Aluminum foil

- Large mixing bowl or small paint bucket, wooden paint stick
- Spatula
- Centimeter ruler
- Laboratory apron, disposable vinyl or latex gloves, safety goggles
- *Geologic Timetable* reference scale

PROCEDURES

1. Mix the plaster of paris according to the manufacturer's directions. Continue to add small amounts of water to achieve a uniform consistency, without lumps. Check with your teacher to be certain that the plaster is ready to use. ⑤ **You should wear disposable gloves and a laboratory apron to protect your skin and clothing.**

2. Carefully pour this mixture into a 9-inch disposable aluminum pan. Then, cover it with aluminum foil. Let this mixture slowly settle, gently shifting the pan back and forth on your table top to achieve an even mixing. Use your spatula to smooth out the top, if necessary.

3. Remove the aluminum foil cover. Then, use a spatula to lightly score the surface of plaster down the middle, producing two equal halves. Each half of the plaster will be for a different dinosaur species, simulating the walking stride, or **dino-tracks**. Be certain to mark each half to keep track of each dinosaur *species.*

4. Obtain two different dinosaur models from your teacher.

(continued)

How Do We Analyze Fossil Tracks in the Rock Record? *(continued)*

5. Write down the species of your model dinosaurs in the appropriate space in Data Table 1 of the Data Collection and Analysis section.

6. To obtain walking-stride footprints, gently press the feet of your first dinosaur model into the left side of the setting plaster close to the edge of the pan. Continue this process, pivoting your model to simulate a *realistic* walking action. Wipe off the excess plaster from your model, and rinse with running water.

7. Repeat the procedure outlined above for your second dinosaur model, using the right side of the plaster-filled pan.

8. After the plaster has completely hardened (set), carefully outline the dinosaur footprints with a fine felt-tip marker.

9. Sketch one set of dinosaur tracks each in Figures 2 and 3 of the Data Collection and Analysis section.

10. Use a *Geologic Timetable* to identify the **era** and **period** when each of your dinosaur species first appeared on Earth. Then, find out when it thrived as a dominant species. Record these findings in the appropriate spaces in Data Table 1.

11. Measure the length (in centimeters) of the walking stride of the first model dinosaur. To do this, follow these steps:

    (a) Measure the stride length as shown in Figure 1.

    (b) Repeat this procedure for each of the steps in your set of tracks.

    (c) Determine the average length of the scaled walking stride for this species: Add up all of the individual lengths that you calculated; then, divide this value by the number of strides in your sample.

    (d) Record the average walking stride length measurement in the appropriate space in Data Table 1. This is a scaled-down version of the stride, since you are using a model that is extremely small compared to the size of the actual organism.

12. Measure the length (in centimeters) of the walking stride of the second model dinosaur by repeating all the procedures outlined in Step 11, using the set of **dino-tracks** from the right side of the plaster cast.

Figure 1

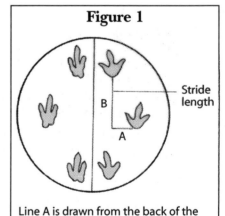

Line A is drawn from the back of the right footprint parallel to the rear of the left footprint. Line B is the perpendicular representing the stride length.

(continued)

Walch Hands-on Science Series: Rocks and Minerals

How Do We Analyze Fossil Tracks in the Rock Record? *(continued)*

13. Transfer all related data (dinosaur species and scaled walking-stride values) from Data Table 1 to their respective columns in Data Table 2 of the Data Collection and Analysis section.

14. Calculate the *approximate* length of the actual walking stride of the first dinosaur species using the following conversion scale:

> **Conversion Scale: 1 cm = 5 feet**

Multiply the average walking distance measured from your footprint tracks by five feet for each centimeter. Record this approximate average of actual walking-stride length measurements for the first dinosaur species in the appropriate space in Data Table 2.

15. Calculate the *approximate* length of the actual walking stride of your second dinosaur species using the same conversion scale listed in step 14. Record this *approximate* average of walking-stride length measurements for the second dinosaur species in the appropriate space in Data Table 2.

 DATA COLLECTION AND ANALYSIS

DATA TABLE 1: RESULTS OF STUDYING A FOSSIL DINOSAUR TRACKS MODEL

Dinosaur Species	Era (1st Appeared/ Dominant)	Period (1st Appeared/ Dominant)	Average Walking-Stride Length (in cm.)

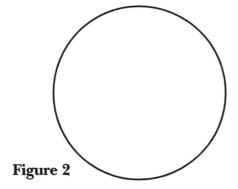

Figure 2

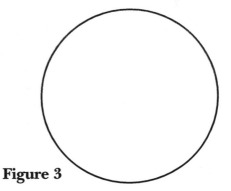

Figure 3

(continued)

How Do We Analyze Fossil Tracks in the Rock Record? *(continued)*

DATA TABLE 2: MEASURING THE STRIDE OF A FOSSIL DINOSAUR TRACKS MODEL

Dinosaur Species	Average Walking-Stride Length, Scaled (in cm.)	Converted Actual Walking-Stride Length (in feet)

❓ CONCLUDING QUESTIONS

1. Why did you need to take the average of the walking stride measurements of the model dinosaurs? _____
_____
_____
_____

2. Compare the "tracks" of your two model dinosaur species. Explain one possible reason for the difference in the walking strides of any two distinct species. _____
_____
_____
_____

3. Assuming your specimen was able to take one step per second, calculate the walking speed of your dinosaur species (in miles per hour). To do this, you need to use conversion factors for distance (1 mile = 5,280 feet) and time (1 hour = 3,600 seconds). _____
_____
_____
_____

▓▓ Follow-up Activity ▓▓

Prepare another version of a plaster cast displaying footprints from several dinosaur species engaged in a battle or some other scenario. You can position them as they walk, run, jump, and so forth. Use this to illustrate that preserved footprints can tell a story, yet be open to interpretation. Write a description of the tale you see preserved in the geological rock record.

Share Your Bright Ideas

We want to hear from you!

Your name_____Date_____

School name_____

School address_____

City _____State _____Zip_____Phone number (_____)_____

Grade level(s) taught_____Subject area(s) taught_____

Where did you purchase this publication?_____

In what month do you purchase a majority of your supplements?_____

What moneys were used to purchase this product?

___School supplemental budget   ___Federal/state funding   ___Personal

Please "grade" this Walch publication in the following areas:

Quality of service you received when purchasing ....A B C D

Ease of use...A B C D

Quality of content...A B C D

Page layout ....A B C D

Organization of material ....A B C D

Suitability for grade level ....A B C D

Instructional value..A B C D

COMMENTS:_____

_____

What specific supplemental materials would help you meet your current—or future—instructional needs?

_____

Have you used other Walch publications? If so, which ones?_____

May we use your comments in upcoming communications?   ___Yes   ___No

Please **FAX** this completed form to **888-991-5755**, or mail it to

   Customer Service, Walch Publishing, P. O. Box 658, Portland, ME 04104-0658

We will send you a **FREE GIFT** in appreciation of your feedback. **THANK YOU!**